THE BOHANNON WITCHES COOKBOOK

EMILY BEX AMY SMITH

Foundations Book Publishing
4209 Lakeland Drive, #398, Flowood, MS 39232
www.FoundationsBooks.net

The Bohannon Witches Cookbook
Emily Bex and Amy Smith

ISBN: 978-1-64583-032-0
Design and Cover:
Dawné Dominique Copyright © 2023

Edited by: Keri Ranger

Introduction

Message from Emily: While writing the *Bohannon Witches Duology*, I found myself going into great detail about what the sisters were cooking up in the kitchen. Perhaps I was hungry at the time. Granted, I was describing meals I'd love to eat. However, I'm no cook! I'm proficient in microwave only. But the idea stuck in my head. *"What about a Bohannon cookbook as a companion to the series?"*

In the Bohannon books, two of the sisters are on a quest to find a grimoire, a one-of-a-kind hand-written journal of spells, with instructions written out for what a witch would need to cast the spell as well as instructions on how to cast it…like a recipe.

Then the idea expanded. What about a cookbook and grimoire combined? I could create the grimoire pages, but there was just one problem, as I said. I'm no cook. I don't even own a cookbook. But luckily for me, my sister Amy is an excellent cook. She had been creating her own recipes for years, as well as collecting recipes handed down from the family. She had mentioned in the past that she'd love to have them published. Hmm. Sounds like the perfect collaboration to me!

What we created is a unique and beautiful cookbook that is a work of art, illustrated with fun 'facts' about the ingredients used to prepare these delicious meals. And like the Bohannon's, never underestimate what a little sister power can do!

Message from Amy: A cookbook for people who don't love to cook? Yep, that's basically the point of this cookbook. I don't actually love to cook. My cooking philosophy is that recipes have to be easy, have relatively few ingredients, and don't require hours spent in the kitchen. I want variety, and I want healthy, well-balanced meals made with fresh ingredients. These are my favorite recipes that have been collected from various sources for more than 35 years. Some are my own creations, and a handful have been passed down from our mother and grandmothers. I did include a few that are more time-consuming, but they're so delicious that it's worth the effort on occasion. The good news is that may of these recipes are great reheated, so if you have leftovers, you don't have to cook every night. Yay!

Penzey's Spices (www.penzeys.com)
- Sandwich Sprinkle
- FoxPoint Seasoning
- Cajun Seasoning
- Tuscan Spice Seasoning
- Chicken Stock Base

Pampered Chef (www.pamperedchef.com)
Rosemary Herb Seasoning

Table of Contents

SANDWICHES

ENTREES

HOLIDAY DISHES

DESSERTS

Breakfast

Cilantro

Protection of gardeners;
Brings peace to the home
and helps to attune one
with their soul.

Associations:

HEALING,
MONEY, SPELLS,
MARS, AND FIRE

Make-Ahead Breakfast Enchiladas

Yield: 10 Enchiladas
Does not reheat well

- 2 cups deli ham, chopped into small pieces
- ½ cup diced green onions
- 2 ½ cups shredded cheddar cheese; divided
- 10 (8-inch) flour tortillas
- 1 ¼ cups half-and-half
- 4 large eggs
- ½ tsp salt
- 1 TBSP flour
- Salsa, sour cream, and extra green onions for serving

Coat a 9×13-inch baking dish with nonstick cooking spray.

Mix the ham, green onions, and 2 cups of cheese in a medium bowl. Scoop ⅓ cup of the blended mixture onto each tortilla; roll up and place seam side down in the baking dish.

Whisk together the half-and-half, eggs, salt, and flour. Pour the liquid over the tortillas. Cover with aluminum foil and refrigerate overnight.

In the morning, preheat the oven to 350° F. Bake with the foil covering for 35 minutes. Remove foil and sprinkle the remaining ½ cup of cheese over the enchiladas. Bake uncovered for 10 more minutes or until the tops are golden brown and the egg mixture is set.

Serve with salsa, sour cream, and additional green onions or cilantro.

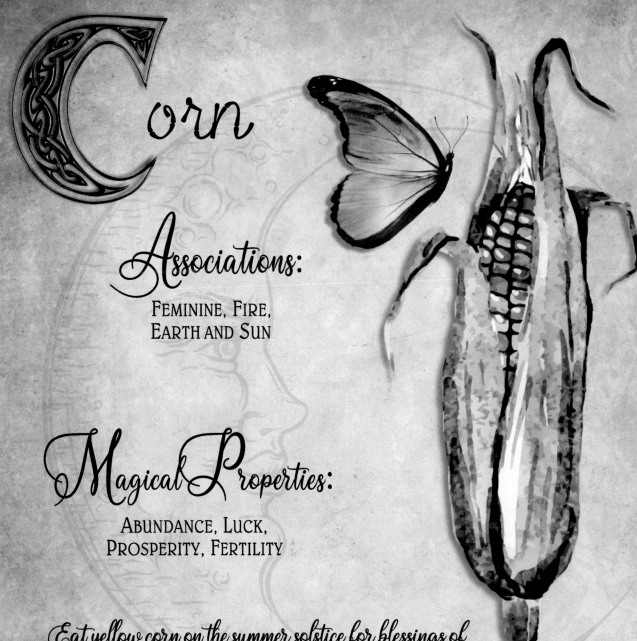

Corn

Associations:

FEMININE, FIRE,
EARTH AND SUN

Magical Properties:

ABUNDANCE, LUCK,
PROSPERITY, FERTILITY

Eat yellow corn on the summer solstice for blessings of
prosperity, consume white corn for spiritual insight,
scatter blue cornmeal to purify and bless a space,
and hang red corn above doorways at harvest time
to protect rewards that have been reaped.

CREAMY CHEESE GRITS

Yield: 6 Servings
Reheats well

- 2 cups beef stock, unsalted
- 4 TBSP organic butter
- 1 cup white or yellow stone ground grits (no instant or quick grits)
- 1 tsp Kosher salt
- 1 cup heavy cream
- ½ cup of water
- 1 cup shredded Cheddar cheese
- Crumbled bacon, optional topping
- Whole kernel corn, optional topping

Add the stock and the butter to a medium-sized saucepan. Turn the heat to medium-high. When the butter begins to melt, add in the grits and salt. Stir well and reduce the heat to low.

After about 12-15 minutes, the grits will start to release puffs of steam. Add the cream and stir well. Continue to stir occasionally for the next 12-15 minutes. Stir in the water and continue occasionally stirring for the next 10 minutes until all liquid is absorbed. The grits should be super creamy.

Remove from heat and stir in the shredded Cheddar.

Serve hot, topped with some shredded cheese, bacon crumbles, and a bit of whole kernel corn.

Leftovers: Pour leftovers into a baking dish, smooth out like bread or cake batter, cover, and refrigerate. To reheat, cut refrigerated grits into square "patties" and sauté them in a skillet with a bit of olive oil or butter.

Wheat (flour)

Sheaves of wheat placed in the home attract money and abundance.

Associations:

Venus, Earth, Abundance, Fertility, Money, Rebirth

Magical Properties:

Wheat is the most sacred of the Seven Sacred Grains as it represents fruitfulness, bounty, and rebirth in its ability to replenish itself and its golden color.

Buttermilk Biscuits

Yield: 12 Biscuits
Reheats well

- ½ cup butter (1 stick), frozen
- 2 ½ cups self-rising flour
- 1 cup chilled buttermilk
- Parchment paper
- 2 TBSP butter, melted

Preheat the oven to 475° F. Grate frozen butter using the large holes of a box grater. Toss together grated butter and flour in a medium bowl. Chill 10 minutes.

Make a well in the center of the mixture. Add buttermilk, and stir 15 times. The dough will be sticky.

Turn dough out onto a lightly floured surface. Lightly sprinkle flour over the top of the dough. Using a lightly floured rolling pin, roll dough into a ¾-inch-thick rectangle (about 9 x 5 inches). Fold dough in half, so short ends meet. Repeat the rolling and folding process 4 more times.

Roll dough to ½-inch thickness. Cut with a 2 ½-inch floured round cutter, reshaping scraps and flouring as needed.

Place dough rounds on a parchment paper-lined baking sheet. Bake at 475° F for 15 minutes or until lightly browned. Brush with melted butter.

Butter

Associations:

FEMININE / RECEPTIVE,
WATER, EARTH, MOON,
ASTROLOGY: CANCER

Magical Properties:

*Sooths relationships, makes things easier,
increases spirituality, smooth's way for spells for peace.*

Ricotta Pancakes

Yield: Approximately 15 Pancakes
Does not reheat well

- 32 oz whole milk Ricotta cheese (about 4 cups) 900 grams
- 1 egg
- ½ - ¾ cup granulated sugar
- 1 ½ cups all-purpose flour + more for shaping the Ricotta pancakes
- ½ tsp baking powder
- 1 tsp vanilla extract (optional)
- Olive oil or butter for frying

Combine 32 oz of Ricotta cheese with 1 egg and mix until the egg is well incorporated (if using vanilla, add 1 tsp vanilla with the egg); add ½ - ¾ cup sugar and mix again; add 1½ cups flour and ½ tsp baking powder and with a minimal amount of mixing bring everything together into a smooth mass.

Using a tablespoon or a large ice cream scoop, scoop the mixture, then drop it into the flour. Coat the ball in flour, then gently shape it into a flat patty about ½ inch thick. You can shape them all and then fry the ricotta pancakes, or shape enough to fill the pan, and while they're frying, continue shaping the rest.

Add about 1 tablespoon of oil to a skillet and heat over low-medium heat. Add ricotta pancakes in, cover with a lid and fry for about 2-3 minutes per side or until well browned on both sides.

To serve: serve warm with a side of sour cream and a jam of choice.

To make the sour cream topping: Combine sour cream with a bit of sugar to make it slightly sweetened. Add more or less sugar to your liking. I do about ½ cup of sour cream plus 1- 2 tablespoons of sugar.
.

Avocados

Grow a plant from the pit of an avocado in your home to bring love into it. Eat the fruit of the avocado to become infused with lust!

Kitchen Witchery:

Use this rich, creamy fruit in the kitchen to "smooth things over" in a tumultuous relationship. Leave a bowl of avocados on the table of an unsettled household, or bring a basket of them to a friend after a difficult discussion to soothe tempers.

Fried Egg & Avocado Toast

Yield: 2 Servings
Does not reheat well

- 2 slices of bread, toasted
- 2 TBSP of butter
- 2 eggs
- 1 avocado, pitted, scooped, and mashed into a bowl
- ¼ cup cherry tomatoes, halved
- Salt and pepper to taste

Pit and scoop avocado and mash with a fork in a small bowl, and season with salt and pepper to taste. Toast bread slices in the toaster while frying the eggs in butter.

Spread avocado over toast slices, top each slice of toast with a fried egg and sprinkle tomato halves on top.

Cloves

Courage Spells:

Carry three clove buds to fill your aura with courage and strength.

Love Spells:

Steep cloves in wine to add romance to your evening.

Wealth Spells:

Sprinkle the ground spice into your wallet to pull wealth into your life.

Luck Spells:

Create a good luck charm by adding cloves, cinnamon, bay, basil, and your favorite good luck herbs to a green sachet bag. Visualize success!

Anxiety Relief:

Diffuse clove essential oil during meditation and mental health healing rituals.

Anya's Pumpkin Muffins

Yield: 12 Muffins

- 1¾ cups all-purpose flour
- 1 cup granulated sugar
- ½ cup brown sugar
- 1 tsp baking soda
- 1 tsp baking powder
- 1 tsp salt
- 2 tsp ground cinnamon
- ¼ tsp ground cloves
- ¼ tsp ground nutmeg
- 2 large eggs
- 1 15 oz can pure pumpkin puree
- 1 cup coconut oil, melted
- 1 TBSP whole milk
- 1 tsp vanilla extract

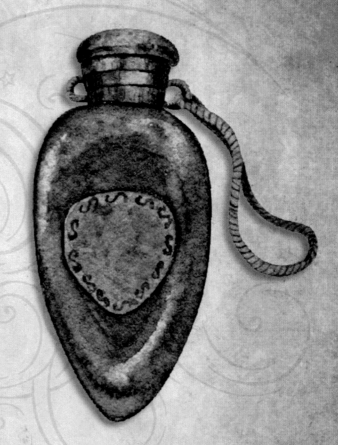

Preheat oven to 375° F.

Line a muffin pan with paper liners or grease with nonstick spray. Set aside.

Combine flour, sugar, brown sugar, baking soda, baking powder, salt, and spices in a medium bowl. Whisk to combine and set aside.

Combine the eggs, pumpkin puree, coconut oil, milk, and vanilla extract in a small bowl. Whisk to combine. Pour the wet mixture into the dry mixture and fold to combine. The batter will be thick.

Using an ice cream scoop, scoop the batter into the prepared muffin pan.

Bake for 22 - 24 minutes or until toothpick inserted into the center of a muffin comes out clean. Let cool for at least 5 minutes before removing muffins from the pan.

Eggs

The egg symbolizes the Spring Equinox when Ostara is celebrated and represents the renewal of life in the natural world.

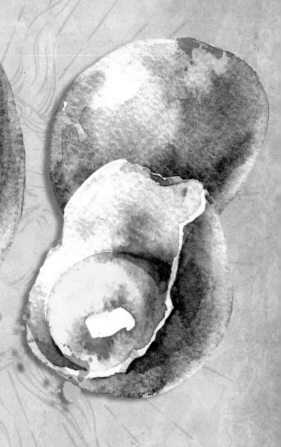

During Ostara, write a wish on a hardboiled egg, then leave it in the woods or natural setting as an offering.

Include eggs in recipes for abundance, fertility, or celebrate the Spring Equinox. Get creative! Scramble, boil, devil, or bake them in quiches. Eat eggs and have breakfast for dinner on the eve of the Spring Equinox for a traditional way to celebrate Ostara.

Mini Breakfast Quiches

Yield: 12 Quiches
Reheats well for 20-30 seconds in microwave

- 12 eggs
- 1½ - 2 cups of your favorite omelet veggies, chopped
- ½ cup chopped ham (optional)
- 1 cup of your favorite omelet cheese, shredded
- Butter or cooking spray
- Salt and pepper to taste
- 12 cup muffin pan

Preheat oven to 375° F.

Grease a muffin pan with butter or cooking spray and set aside.

In a large bowl, beat eggs with a whisk. Set aside.

Chop 1½ - 2 cups of your favorite omelet veggies and lightly sauté in butter over medium heat until crisp-tender (onions, mushrooms, peppers, for example).

Place equal portions of veggies in each muffin cup and top each with chopped ham and a sprinkle of cheese. Pour egg into each cup to fill.

Bake at 375° F for 15 - 20 minutes or until set.

Chives

Keep a bundle of chives (or growing in a pot) tied with a black ribbon near the front door to ward off evil spirits and negative people.

To bring more money into the house, tie a chive blade around a note of currency while you chant, "Money come to me. I do not ask for much you see, just so my needs are met, so this magic is set." Leave it in the area of the house where you need the money (the kitchen if you need a new fridge, etc.), and leave it there until the chive dries out. It is believed the money should come to you.

Sausage Pinwheels

Yield: Approx. 12 Pinwheels
Reheats well for 20 - 30 seconds in microwave

- 1 tube Pillsbury® Refrigerated Crescent Dinner Rolls
- ½ lb uncooked bulk pork sausage
- 2 TBSP minced chives

Preheat oven to 375° F.

Unroll crescent roll dough on a lightly floured surface and press seams and perforations together. Roll into a 14 x 10 rectangle. Spread sausage to within ½ inch of the edges of the dough. Sprinkle with chives. Carefully roll up from a long side and cut into 12 fairly equal slices.

Place 1 inch apart on an un-greased baking sheet (you can line it with parchment paper if you prefer). Bake for 12 - 16 minutes or until golden brown.

Parsley

Attributes:

PURIFICATION, REBIRTH
PROTECTION, AND
CLEANSING

Magical Properties:

Parsley is a potent protector. Place parsley seeds around your home to protect you from negative energy. Make an amulet with dried parsley seeds and wear it close to your heart to attract love and fertility into your life.

Sausage Balls

Yield: Approximately 30 sausage balls
Reheats well

- 1 lb ground pork sausage, mild
- 2 cups Bisquick®
- 4 cups shredded sharp Cheddar cheese
- 2 TBSP parsley
- 1 tsp paprika
- ½ tsp black pepper
- Olive oil

Preheat the oven to 350° F and line a baking sheet with parchment paper.

In a large bowl, mix all ingredients except olive oil. This mixture is supposed to be crumbly.

Use olive oil to moisten the palms of your hands and create tablespoon-size balls with the sausage mixture, and place them on a baking sheet. Don't pack the balls too tight, or they won't cook through.

Bake until deeply golden and no longer pink, about 25 - 30 minutes.

These are obviously great for breakfast but are also a great appetizer. For an occasional change, use store-bought apricot marmalade, at room temperature, as a dipping sauce.

Salads

Honey

Use honey as a natural cough aid.

Honey is an excellent preservative and has strong antibacterial properties, making it an ideal addition to any salves.

Try to source local honey; this also helps with seasonal allergies!

Caprese Salad with Balsamic Vinaigrette

Yield: 4 Servings

- 1 large bunch of fresh basil leaves (⅓ cup)
- 12 - 16 oz fresh Mozzarella cheese, sliced ¼ inch thick
- 3 - 4 Roma tomatoes, sliced ¼ inch thick
- 3 TBSP olive oil
- 3 TBSP balsamic vinegar
- 1½ TBSP honey

Wash basil leaves, pat dry, and place leaves on a medium-size platter. Place Mozzarella slices on top of the basil, then place tomato slices on the mozzarella.

Mix olive oil, balsamic vinegar, and honey in a small bowl until well blended. Plate salads individually and drizzle the dressing on each salad.

Symbols of Rhiannon

White Horse

Birds

Moon

Gates

Apple Slaw

Yield: 6 Servings
This is an excellent, healthy side dish for burgers, hot dogs, and sandwiches.

- 1 bag Dole® Classic Coleslaw, washed
- 1 Fuji apple, washed, and cut into bite-size pieces
- 1 bunch of green onions, washed and sliced
- ¼ cup Ken's Steak House® Lite Sweet Vidalia Onion Dressing

Pour half of the Coleslaw mix into a colander and rinse. Let sit to drain.

Chop apple and green onions.

In a large mixing bowl, add the coleslaw, apple pieces, and onions, and stir in ¼ cup of Sweet Vidalia Onion Dressing.

Onions

White onions clear away obstacles
when peeled to the core.

Yellow onions dispel anger
between friends.

Use purple onions for power
and seduction.

Red onions promote lust when added to dishes.

Southwest Chicken Salad

Yield: 4 Servings

- 1 store-bought roasted chicken (chicken removed from the bone and cut into bite-size pieces)
- 1 head of leaf or romaine lettuce
- 1 small onion, sliced, rings separated
- 1 small green pepper
- 1 carrot, sliced
- 1 15 oz. can of corn, drained
- 1 15 oz. can of black beans, drained
- ¾ cups Sharp Cheddar cheese, shredded
- ¼ cup Hidden Valley® Ranch Dressing
- ¼ cup of your favorite barbeque sauce

In a small bowl, mix Ranch dressing and barbeque sauce. Set aside.

Wash and chop lettuce, onion, green pepper, and carrot. Assemble in a large salad bowl, top with chicken, add drained corn and back beans, and top with cheddar cheese. Drizzle individual servings with Ranch-barbeque dressing.

Pears

Pears represent longevity, purity, wisdom, grace, and nobility. There are many legends about how this fruit enhances female fertility.

Due to their feminine shape, pears are often used in love and lust spells. Serve pears to the one you desire, or carry dried pear pieces in charm bags. Spray on a little pear-scented perfume as a sweet aphrodisiac!

Pear Salad with Candied Walnuts & Cranberries

Yield: 8 Servings

Balsamic Vinaigrette
- ⅓ cup extra virgin olive oil
- 2½ TBSP balsamic vinegar
- 1 TBSP honey
- 1 tsp Dijon mustard
- 1½ TBSP finely diced shallots
- Salt and freshly ground black pepper

Salad
- ½ cup walnuts
- 1 TBSP salted butter
- 1 TBSP packed light-brown sugar
- 7 oz pkg Spring Mix® Salad & Spinach blend
- 2 oz Parmesan cheese, shaved or shredded
- 2 pears, sliced thin (Bartlett or Anjou are great)
- ⅓ cup Ocean Spray® Craisins (dried cranberries)

In a small lidded bowl, add olive oil, balsamic vinegar, honey, Dijon mustard, diced shallots, salt, and pepper to taste. Mix well, cover, and place in the refrigerator.

In a medium skillet, melt the butter along with brown sugar over medium heat. Once the mixture has melted, add walnuts and cook, constantly stirring, until caramelized, about 2 minutes. Transfer to a plate in a single layer to cool.

Layer lettuce then pears in a large bowl and top with Parmesan, dried cranberries, and candied walnuts. Drizzle plated servings with chilled balsamic vinaigrette.

Mustard Seeds

Carry in a mojo bag along with other herbs and talismans.

Add to a bath for spiritual cleansing.

Yellow mustard seeds are used to bring good luck and protect against negativity. They guard against evil, restore virility, and aid in love spells.

Tuna Pasta Salad

Yield: 4 Servings

- 1 12 oz can of tuna, packed in water, drained
- 2 eggs, hard-boiled
- ½ cup Ditalini pasta, cooked
- ¼ cup chopped onion
- ½ tsp black pepper
- 1 TBSP yellow mustard
- ⅓ cup olive oil mayonnaise

Hard boil the eggs, peel, and chop.

Cook pasta according to package directions and drain.

Chop onion.

In a medium-sized bowl, mix drained tuna, drained cooked pasta, chopped eggs, chopped onions, pepper, mustard, and mayonnaise.

Great served on a bed of lettuce. Great sides with this recipe are apple slices or a handful of grapes, a few cheese cubes, and garlic rolls.

Cabbage

Cabbage should be planted in the garden first thing after a couple has been wed if they wish to have good luck in their marriage and their garden

Attributes:

Feminine,
Moon, Water,
Luck

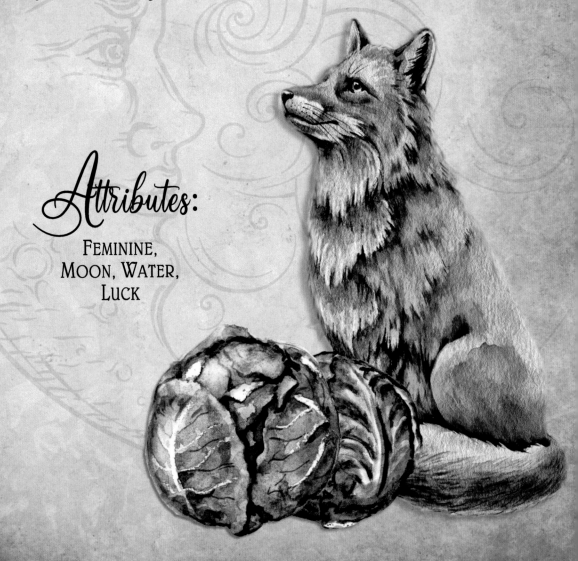

Chinese Coleslaw

Yield: 6 Servings

- 1 bag Dole® Classic Coleslaw
- 1 cup chopped red cabbage
- 1 bunch of green onions, sliced
- ⅓ cup store-bought peanut sauce

Wash coleslaw mix and pat dry with paper towels. Chop and wash red cabbage and pat dry. Chop green onions.

In a medium bowl, combine veggies and stir in peanut sauce.

Cranberries

Love: Cook with cranberries to inspire love.

Healing: Place cranberries in a bowl and place the bowl under the bed during healing or rest.

Energy: Make homemade cranberry sauce with cinnamon and clove for increasing energy.

Cranberries' Medicinal Properties have been effective against urinary tract infections.

Mandarin Orange Cranberry Salad

Yield: 6 - 8 Servings

- 1 head of red leaf or Romaine lettuce
- 1 small onion, sliced into rings and separated
- 1 carrot, peeled and sliced thin
- ½ cup dried Ocean Spray® cranberries
- 1 small can of Dole® Mandarin oranges in light syrup, drained
- ¼ cup slivered almonds
- ⅓ cup sharp Cheddar cheese, shredded
- Wishbone® Red Wine Vinaigrette

Wash and prepare vegetables. Layer lettuce, onions, carrots, cranberries, Mandarin oranges, and almonds in a large salad bowl. Top with Cheddar cheese. Drizzle plated portions with red wine vinaigrette.

ears

Pears represent longevity, purity, wisdom, grace, and nobility. There are many legends about how this fruit enhances female fertility.

Due to their feminine shape, pears are often used in love and lust spells. Serve pears to the one you desire, or carry dried pear pieces in charm bags. Spray on a little pear-scented perfume as a sweet aphrodisiac!

Peach & Boiled Peanut Salad

Yield: 6 Servings

- 1 head Romaine or red leaf lettuce
- 2 - 3 fresh sliced peaches
- 1 small onion, sliced into rings and separated
- 1 can of Peanut Patch® Boiled Peanuts, drained (Kroger or Amazon)
- Briana's® Poppyseed Salad Dressing

Wash lettuce and pat dry. Tear or chop into bite-size pieces. Place in a large salad bowl.

Place sliced onions rings on top of lettuce.

Wash and slice peaches and place on top of onions.

Drain canned peanuts and scatter them over top of peaches.

Drizzle each plated salad with Briana's® Poppyseed Dressing.

Apples

Attributes:
Love, Spirituality, Knowledge, Wisdom, Fertility

Associations:
Taurus. Venus. Used during Mabon and Samhain rituals.

Apples deepen your spiritual connection to the earth. Cut an apple crosswise to reveal a pentagram. Eat an apple before meditation to connect to ancient wisdom.

Apple Walnut Salad with Balsamic Vinaigrette

Yield: 6 Servings

- 1 head red leaf lettuce
- 1 apple, sliced thin
- 1 small onion, sliced into rings
- ½ cup shredded white Cheddar cheese
- ¼ cup walnuts

Balsamic Vinaigrette

- 4 TBSP Pompeian® or Colavita® Balsamic Vinegar
- 2 TBSP olive oil
- 2 TBSP honey

Layer salad starting with lettuce, then add onions, apple slices, walnuts, and cheddar cheese.

Mix balsamic vinegar, olive oil and honey in a small bowl. Drizzle over the individually plated salads.

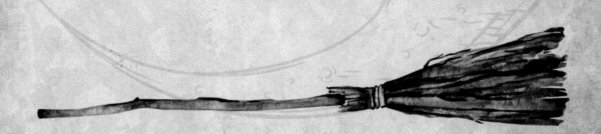

Cucumbers

Attributes:
Venus, Moon, Libra, Taurus, Aphrodite.

Fertility:
Carry a cucumber with you when trying to conceive to help balance your feminine energies with masculine energies.

Healing:
In ancient times, these were used to heal swelling, exhaustion, hangovers, and much more! Eat them when you are feeling ill.

Antipasto Salad

Yield: 6 Servings

- 1 cucumber, peeled and sliced
- 1 red onion, sliced into rings
- ½ cup pitted ripe black olives, sliced
- 2 plum or Roma tomatoes, sliced
- 2 oz thinly sliced salami, cut into fourths
- 1 head red leaf lettuce
- ¾ cup fresh grated Parmesan cheese
- Your favorite Italian salad dressing

Wash and prepare all veggies. Layer salad starting with lettuce, followed by cucumber, red onion, tomatoes, salami, black olives, and Parmesan.

Dress with Italian dressing on individual plated servings.

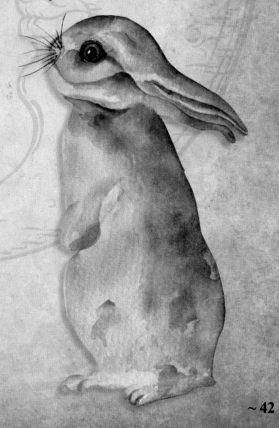

Thyme

Associations:

VENUS, AIR,
WATER, AND CAPRICORN

Attributes:

PURITY, HEALING,
COURAGE, AND STRENGTH

Add fresh or dried thyme to your ritual bath water
to aid in the release of burdensome emotions. Keep a
sprig of thyme in your wallet to invite abundance.
Add a drop of thyme oil to your pillow to attract
insightful dreams.

Blackened Chicken Salad

Yield: 6 Servings
Spicy

- 1 TBSP paprika
- 1 tsp onion powder
- 1 tsp garlic powder
- ½ tsp oregano
- ½ tsp thyme
- ½ tsp white pepper
- ½ tsp ground red pepper
- ½ tsp ground black pepper
- 1 lb boneless, skinless chicken breasts
- 4 TBSP melted butter
- 4 cups bite-size pieces of fresh spinach leaves
- 2 cups bite-size pieces of Romaine lettuce
- 2 cups zucchini, cubed
- 2 cups cucumber, cubed
- ½ cup sliced green onion
- 1 medium tomato, cut into eight wedges
- 1 bag of garlic butter croutons
- Hidden Valley Ranch® Buttermilk Dressing

Preheat oven to 350° F.

In a small bowl, mix all spices together to create a rub for the chicken. Wash chicken and place in a baking dish. Drizzle with melted butter and sprinkle with the spice mixture. Bake 50 - 60 minutes.

Wash and prepare all vegetables and layer them into a large salad bowl.

When chicken is done and cooled, cut into bite-size pieces and add to the top of the salad. Add croutons. Dress plated individual servings with Ranch dressing.

Pecans

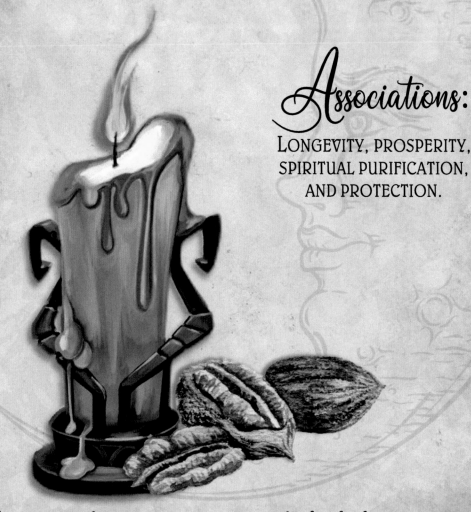

Associations:
LONGEVITY, PROSPERITY,
SPIRITUAL PURIFICATION,
AND PROTECTION.

When you crack open a pecan to eat, speak aloud what you are grateful for. This simple act of gratitude will draw more abundance and prosperity towards you.

Peach & Pecan Salad

Yield: 6 Servings

- 2 - 3 fresh peaches, sliced
- 1 head red leaf lettuce
- 1 small onion, sliced into rings
- ¼ cup candied pecans
- ¼ cup shredded Mozzarella cheese
- Store bought honey-mustard salad dressing

Wash and prepare peaches and vegetables. Layer in a large salad bowl, starting with lettuce, onions, peaches, pecans, and Mozzarella. Dress with honey-mustard salad dressing once individually plated.

If you can't find candied pecans, pour pecans onto a lined baking sheet, drizzle with melted butter and sprinkle with brown sugar (a little cinnamon, if you like), and bake at 350° F for about 10 minutes.

Soups

Ginger Root

Inspire passion and bring "heat" into a relationship with the help of ginger in a spell bag.

Attributes:

PASSION, LOVE, MONEY, HEALING, LUCK, AND ENERGY

Feeling sheepish before a big presentation? In need of a dose of bravery before a first date? If you plan to go way outside your comfort zone, chew on some ginger root beforehand to stir your courage.

Simple Chicken Soup

Yield: 6 Servings
Reheats well

- 2 - 3 boneless, skinless, chicken breasts
- 2 carrots, peeled and sliced into discs
- 2 stalks of celery, chopped
- 1 small onion, chopped (about a cup)
- 1 small piece of ginger root, peeled and cut into ½ inch chunks
- 1 (32oz.) box Kitchen Basics® or similar brand chicken stock (or broth)
- 1 TBSP Penzey's® Tuscan Sunset Seasoning
- Salt and pepper to taste
- 1 TBSP olive oil
- Water to cover the chicken by 2 - 3 inches

Boil chicken in salted water for one hour in a large stock pot. Remove chicken and cut into small, bite-sized pieces and set aside.

Discard water from the stock pot and add 1 TBSP olive oil. Sauté vegetables for 2 to 3 minutes. Add chicken, chicken stock, ginger root, and Tuscan Sunset Seasoning. Bring to a boil, reduce heat and simmer for 45 minutes to an hour.

You may wish to remove the ginger root before serving. The ginger gives the soup a great flavor, but some people may not like to eat the actual pieces of ginger root… or you may love it! Explore the mysteries and magic of ginger on your own.

Samhain

Samhain originated from ancient Celtic/Irish spiritual traditions. Samhain (a Gaelic word pronounced ("SAH-win") is celebrated from October 31 to November 1 to welcome in the harvest and usher in the dark half of the year. Wiccans believe that the barriers between the physical world and the spirit world break down during Samhain, allowing more interaction between humans and those who reside in the Summerland. The ritual has been adopted by many for modern-day Halloween celebrations.

Creamy Mushroom, Chicken and Wild Rice Soup

Yield: 8 Servings
Reheats well

- 3 TBSP butter, divided
- 1 lb mushrooms, sliced
- 1 onion, diced
- 2 carrots, diced
- 2 stalks celery, diced
- 2 cloves garlic, chopped
- 1 tsp thyme, chopped
- 6 cups Kitchen Basics® Chicken Stock (2 boxes)
- 1 cup wild rice (or a blend of white rice and wild rice)
- 1½ cups chicken, cooked and diced or shredded
- 1 cup milk or cream
- 1 cup Parmesan cheese, grated
- Salt and pepper to taste
- Extra grated Parmesan for topping, if desired

Melt 2 TBSP butter in a pan over medium-high heat, add the mushrooms, and cook until the mushrooms have released their liquids and the liquid has evaporated, about 10 - 15 minutes. Set aside.

Melt 1 TBSP butter in a Dutch oven or soup pot and add the onions, carrots, and celery and cook until tender, about 8 -10 minutes. Mix in the garlic and thyme and cook until fragrant, about a minute.

Add the broth, rice, chicken, and mushrooms, bring to a boil, reduce the heat, and simmer, covered, until the rice is tender about 20 - 30 minutes.

Mix in the milk or cream and cheese and cook until the cheese has melted; stir in salt and pepper to taste.

 Garlic

Attributes:

PROTECTION, HEALING,
STRENGTH, COURAGE,
AND LUCK

Associations:

FIRE, ARIES,
MARS, MASCULINITY

To repel negative energy, hang a garlic clove on your front door. Carry an
amulet filled with dried garlic for good luck. Carry a clove of garlic in
your pocket to give you strength when facing difficult situations.
(The vampires said to save it for cooking, it does not affect them.)

Creamy Tomato Bisque

Yield: 8 Servings
Reheats well

- 28 oz can Hunt's® Crushed Tomatoes
- 32 oz box Kitchen Basics® Chicken Stock
- 2 TBSP tomato paste
- 1 cup diced onion
- 2 cloves garlic, minced
- 1 TBSP olive oil
- ½ cup heavy whipping cream
- Salt and pepper to taste
- ½ cup shredded extra-sharp Cheddar cheese for topping (optional)

In a large soup pot over medium heat, sauté onions and garlic in olive oil and cook for 3 - 5 minutes.

Add tomato paste, crushed tomatoes, and chicken stock, stirring until well combined. Reduce heat to low and cook for 15 minutes. Add heavy cream and stir until well blended.

Serve and top with a sprinkle of grated Cheddar cheese.

Great served with grilled cheese sandwiches or grilled cheese toast. Also, pretty amazing with garlic bread.

Mozzarella Cheese

Spell-making is based on symbolic parallels, and cheeses yield no shortage of them: The smooth curves of a mozzarella fit in a spell for a healthy childbirth or to comfort a child wrestling with nightmares.

Along an ancient trail in Peeblesshire, Scotland, two rocks mark a spot called the Cheese Well. According to superstition, those who pass by should throw a nibble of cheese into it as an offering to the fairies to whom it belongs.

French Onion Soup Casserole

Yield: 4 Servings
Does not reheat well

- 3 medium sweet onions, sliced
- 3 TBSP butter
- 4 cups beef broth
- 1 tsp Worcestershire® sauce
- 4 oz French baguette bread, sliced about ½-inch in thickness (approximately 10 - 12 small slices)
- 1 cup shredded Mozzarella cheese
- ¼ cup grated Parmesan cheese

Preheat oven to 350° F.

Lightly toast the slices of bread in the toaster and set aside.

Melt butter in a large saucepan over low heat. Add onions and cover. Cook for about 30 minutes, stirring occasionally.

Add the beef broth and the Worcestershire® sauce. Heat the broth mixture until it boils. Reduce heat to low and simmer, uncovered, for about 30 minutes. The broth will reduce.

Pour the onion and broth mixture into a medium-greased casserole dish. Place toasted bread in a single layer on top of onion/broth mixture. Cover the bread with a thick layer of shredded Mozzarella and top with grated Parmesan.

Bake, uncovered, for 20 - 30 minutes or until cheese is melted and brown on top.

Oregano

Associations:

Venus, Air, Femininity, Taurus, Libra

Attributes:

Protection, Creativity, Travel, Freedom, Love, and Happiness

Plant oregano near your front door to protect your home. Sprinkle dried oregano around the perimeter of your home to attract joy and lightness. To make travel easier place a few dried oregano leaves into an amulet or in your shoes. Use oregano in your cooking to inspire uplifting conversations.

Pasta Fagioli

Yield: 12 Servings
Reheats well

Refrigerates and freezes well. Keep the additional beef stock on hand as the pasta sometimes absorbs too much liquid when refrigerated or frozen, so you may need to add more beef stock when reheating.

- 1 lb. ground beef
- 1 cup diced onion
- 1 cup chopped celery
- 2 large carrots, peeled and sliced
- 2 32 oz boxes Kitchen Basics® Beef Stock
- 1 24 oz jar Simply Ragu® Traditional Spaghetti Sauce
- 1 can diced tomatoes
- 1 can light red kidney beans
- 1 can great northern beans
- 1 TBSP dried oregano
- 1 tsp Penzey's® Tuscan Sunset Seasoning
- Salt and pepper to taste
- 8 oz Ditalini pasta (or other small pasta)
- Fresh grated Parmesan cheese

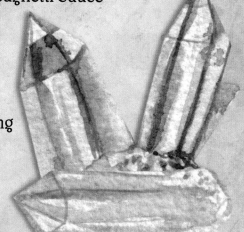

In large stockpot, brown ground beef. Stir in onion, celery, and carrots and cook for another 3 - 5 minutes. Add in 1 box of beef stock, diced tomatoes, spaghetti sauce, beans, and seasonings. Bring to a boil, then reduce heat and simmer for 40 - 45 minutes.

Stir in pasta and cook until pasta is al dente. If the pasta absorbs too much liquid, add more beef stock to desired consistency. But hold onto the remaining beef stock. If it's not needed here, you may need it for the leftovers after the soup has been refrigerated. You won't need the whole box, but this brand has a long shelf life if you refrigerate it after opening it so you can use it in other recipes.

Top each serving with a generous portion of Parmesan cheese.

Great Northern Beans

Beans are powerful symbols that point to increased spiritual growth and psychic power.

If you dreamed of planting a bean, it's possible you are willing to do the hard work now in order to benefit from it in the future.

Bean & Ham Soup

Yield: 6 Servings
Reheats well

- 2 cups cooked ham, chopped
- 1 cup diced onions
- 1 cup diced carrots
- 1 cup diced celery
- 2 cloves garlic, minced
- 3 cups Kitchen Basics® Chicken Stock
- 3 15-oz cans of Great Northern beans
- 1 8-oz can tomato sauce
- Salt and pepper to taste
- 1 TBSP olive oil

Heat olive oil in a large soup pot or Dutch oven over medium heat. Add ham and sauté for 4 - 5 minutes. Stir in veggies and garlic and sauté for another 3 - 4 minutes.

Stir in the beans, chicken stock, and tomato sauce. Season to taste with salt and pepper. Bring to a boil, then reduce heat to low and let the soup simmer for 1 hour.

Cumin

It is used in love spells and promotes fidelity when given to a lover. Cumin seed is steeped in wine to make a lust potion.

Associations:

MASCULINE,
MARS,
FIRE

Magical Uses:

Cumin seed possesses the "gift of retention." It will prevent the theft of any object which retains it. Cumin is burned with frankincense for protection and scattered on the floor, sometimes with salt, to drive out evil. Brides also wear it to keep negativity away from the wedding.

Southwest White Chili

Yield: 6 Servings
Reheats well

- 3 boneless, skinless chicken breasts
- 1 TBSP olive oil
- 1 32 oz box Kitchen Basics® Chicken Stock (have a little extra on hand)
- ¾ cup chopped onion
- 1 green pepper, chopped
- 3 cans Great Northern® Beans
- 1 tsp garlic powder
- 2 tsp ground cumin
- 1 tsp dried oregano
- ½ tsp ground red pepper
- 1 pinch dried cilantro
- 1 cup fresh grated Parmesan cheese
- 1 bag of store-bought garlic butter croutons

Wash chicken and boil in salted water in a large stockpot for 1 hour. Remove chicken and shred or cut it into bite-size pieces. Set aside. Pour out the cooking water.

In the same pot, sauté onion and green pepper in olive oil for about 2 minutes or until softened. Add beans and chicken and stir in enough chicken stock to barely cover everything. This is not as thick as traditional chili but should not be soup-like consistency either. The exact chicken stock quantity may vary each time you make this dish. Sometimes you may need a little less or a little more. The cumin will thicken the liquid a bit in the simmering/cooking process so keep that in mind as well. Pour the stock in slowly so you can gauge consistency and not end up with soup instead of chili.

Stir in spices and bring to a boil. Cover, reduce heat to low, and simmer for 30 minutes, stirring occasionally.

Top each serving with Parmesan cheese, and garlic butter flavored croutons if desired. Monterey Jack cheese is a nice variation if you have it on hand.

Cayenne Pepper

Use in spells to remove obstacles
and blockages that may keep you
from obtaining a specific goal.

Magical Properties:

PROTECTION, STRENGTH,
MOTIVATION, COURAGE;
INCREASES YOUR AURA.

Some say red pepper can be added to love spells to "spice things up."
But don't use too much, or that spice could lead to endless fights!

Slightly Sweet & Spicy Chili

Yield: 8 Servings
Reheats well

- 1 lb lean ground beef
- 1 cup chopped onion
- 2 cloves garlic, minced
- ¼ tsp salt
- 1 40 oz can Hanover® Light Red Kidney Beans (or 3 small cans)
- 1½ cans diced tomatoes
- 1 bay leaf
- 2 TBSP chili powder
- 2 TBSP ground cumin
- 1 TBSP brown sugar
- ¼ tsp cayenne pepper

Brown ground beef in a large soup pot or Dutch oven. Stir in onions, garlic, and salt. Cook 2 - 3 minutes or until veggies are translucent.

Stir in beans, tomatoes, bay leaf, and spices.

Simmer over low heat for 60 - 90 minutes, depending on desired thickness, stirring occasionally.

Great served over rice or topped with your favorite shredded cheese and/or a dollop of sour cream.

Bay Leaf

Attributes:

BANISHING, PROTECTION, BINDING, HEALING, WISDOM

Associations:

SUN, LEO, FIRE, MASCULINITY

Magical Properties:

Use dried bay leaves to purify your home. Keep the leaves under your pillow to invite inspiring dreams. Carry a bay leaf to ward off negative energy.

Hearty Chicken Soup

Yield: 8 - 10 Servings
Reheats well and freezes well

You will need a deep pot for this soup recipe. A normal Dutch oven will work, but it will be filled to the brim.

- 2 - 3 large chicken breasts (bone & skin intact are best, but boneless and skinless are good too)
- 2 32 oz boxes Kitchen Basics® Chicken Stock
- 2 TBSP olive oil
- ½ head of green cabbage, cut into chunks
- 3 carrots, peeled and sliced
- 1 large green pepper, chopped
- 1 small onion, chopped
- 3 cloves garlic, minced
- 1 can of green peas, un-drained
- 1 can diced tomatoes, un-drained
- 2 tsp Penzey's® Chicken Stock Base (or 2 chicken bouillon cubes)
- 1 TBSP dried oregano
- 1 tsp poultry seasoning
- 1 bay leaf
- 2 tsp salt
- 1 tsp black pepper
- ½ cup wild rice
- ½ cup white rice

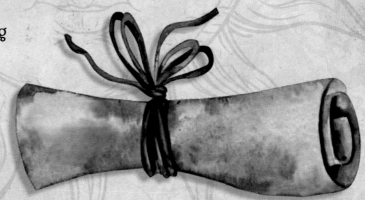

Place washed chicken in a large soup pot. Sprinkle generously with salt. Add water to cover the chicken by about 3 inches. Bring to a boil, then reduce heat to medium, loosely cover with pot lid and let boil for an hour. When chicken is done, remove skin and discard. Remove chicken from bones with a fork, so it looks shredded. If you used boneless breasts, shred the chicken using two forks. Set aside.

Hearty Chicken Soup

Continued...

In the same Dutch oven sauté onions, green pepper, and garlic in olive oil for about 2 minutes. Add carrots, tomatoes, cabbage, chicken, and enough chicken stock to cover. Stir in seasonings and bring to a boil. Reduce heat to low, cover, and simmer for 1 hour or until cabbage is quite limp. Add in peas and cook another 15 minutes.

While soup simmers, cook the white rice and the wild rice according to package directions in separate pans (cooking time is different for each one). When done, stir the two kinds of rice together. Place a serving of rice in each serving bowl, then serve the soup over the rice.

NOTE: This is a unique way of adding rice to your soup. However, this soup takes up so much room in the pot that it's almost impossible to cook it with the rice in it, and the rice absorbs so much of the liquid when cooked that it's hard to determine the right amount of chicken stock needed. You may still want an extra box of chicken stock on hand.

Witchin'
IN THE
KITCHEN

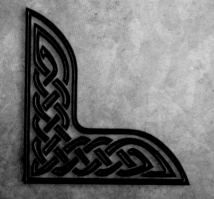

Barley

Barley may be scattered on the ground to keep evil and negativity away.

Associations:

FEMININE, VENUS,
EARTH, LOVE,
HEALING, AND PROTECTION

Magical Uses:

Use the grain or barley water in love spells. If you have a toothache, it can be cured with barley. Wind a barley straw around a stone, visualizing your pain into the stone. Now throw it into a river or any running water, and see your pain being washed away.

Bean & Barley Soup

Yield: 8 Servings
Reheats well

- 1 small bag (12-15 oz) of mixed dried beans
- 2 - 3 cups of water (for soaking beans)
- 1 tsp salt
- 1 cup Quaker® Quick Barley (pearled), cooked
- 1 cup chopped onion
- 3 large carrots, peeled and sliced
- 2 cloves garlic, minced
- 1 - 2 TBSP olive oil
- 20 oz can diced tomatoes
- 32 oz box Kitchen Basics® Beef Stock (but have extra on hand)
- 1 TBSP Italian Seasoning
- 1 TBSP oregano
- 1 tsp celery salt
- 1 tsp black pepper
- 1 bay leaf
- Garlic butter croutons (optional)
- Shredded sharp Cheddar cheese (optional)
- Knorr® Beef Bouillon cubes (have on hand)

Place dried beans in a large Dutch oven and add 2 - 3 cups of water to cover the beans by about 2 inches. Add a tsp of salt and bring to a boil over high heat. Let boil for 5 minutes. Remove from heat and let beans soak for 1 hour. Drain water from beans using a colander and set them aside.

Cook barley according to package directions.

Bean & Barley Soup

Continued...

In the same Dutch oven, heat olive oil over medium heat and sauté onions, garlic, and carrots for about 3 minutes or until they start to soften.

Stir in beans, tomatoes, and cooked barley. Add beef stock and seasonings. Bring to a boil, then reduce heat to simmer. Cover and cook for 90 minutes, stirring occasionally.

NOTE: If the beans absorb too much liquid as they cook, add more beef broth until you reach the desired consistency. If this waters down the broth's flavor, you can add one or two Knorr® Beef Bouillon cubes.

Top individual servings with garlic butter croutons and/or shredded cheese. It's great either way. If there are leftovers, serve it without toppings the first day and with toppings another day to change it up a bit.

Cookin' Something Wicked

Potatoes

Associations:

FEMININE,
EARTH, MOON,
VIRGO

Call stability and protection into your life with the humble potato.

Grounding: *After meditation, eat potatoes to ground yourself back in reality.*

Protection: *Cut a potato into quarters and bury the quarters at the four corners of your property.*

Stability: *When you cook or eat potatoes, visualize stability in your life.*

Baked Potato Soup

Yield: 6 Servings
Reheats well

- 4 large baking potatoes
- ½ cup flour
- 6 cups 2% milk
- 5 oz extra-sharp Cheddar cheese, shredded
- Kosher salt
- Black pepper
- 4 oz sour cream
- 3 TBSP green onions, sliced
- 3 TBSP fresh or dried chives
- 2 TBSP butter
- Garlic butter croutons

Bake potatoes in the microwave, let them cool and cut them into bite-size pieces. It's your choice if you want to leave the skin on or remove it; this recipe is good either way.

Place potatoes in a large soup pot, sprinkle in salt and pepper to taste and add milk and butter. Slowly heat over medium heat without letting it boil.

Add flour slowly, constantly stirring, until all flour has been added and the soup has thickened. Sometimes this takes a while, so be patient.

Serve in individual bowls and top each with a dollop of sour cream, green onions, chives, croutons, and cheese.

Sandwiches

Smudge Sticks

White sage smudge sticks are the best-known ceremonial smudge plant. It can change the mood and energy of a room. It is also used for meditation, cleansing, and purification.

Add some lavender to your white sage to increase your psychic healing and tranquility.

Easy Peanut Chicken Wraps

Yield: 6 Servings

For the Chicken Wraps

- 3 cups coleslaw mix
- 1 cup shredded carrots
- ⅓ cup roasted peanuts
- ¼ cup chopped fresh cilantro
- 2 cooked chicken breasts, chopped or sliced
- 6 large tortillas

For the Peanut Sauce

- ¼ cup honey
- ¼ cup olive oil (or vegetable oil)
- ¼ cup peanut butter
- 3 TBSP unseasoned rice vinegar
- 1 TBSP soy sauce
- 1 tsp sesame oil
- ½ tsp pepper
- ¼ tsp salt
- ¼ - ½ tsp crushed red pepper flakes
- 1 TBSP grated fresh ginger
- 1 large garlic clove, minced

In a medium bowl, whisk together the peanut sauce ingredients.

In another bowl, add the cabbage, carrots, cilantro, and peanuts. Pour the sauce over the mixture and stir. Let this sit while you prepare the tortillas and chicken.

Heat up the tortillas for about 10 seconds in the microwave to make them easier to work with.

Divide the chicken and coleslaw between each tortilla. Roll tightly, securing with toothpicks if necessary. Serve whole, or slice each tortilla into 3-inch mini roll up sandwiches.

Poppy Seed

Poppy seeds are added to food to induce calmness or deepen feelings.

Sleep on a pillow stuffed with poppy seeds to bring relief from insomnia.

To become invisible, soak poppy seeds in wine for fifteen days, then drink the wine over the next five days while fasting. (I think if you drink wine for five days while fasting, you will just feel invisible.)

Ham & Cheese Party Sandwiches

Yield: 12 Servings
Reheats well in oven

- 12 King's® Hawaiian mini sandwich rolls (Substitute: Martin's® Potato rolls)
- ½ - 1 lb deli ham, sliced a little thick (or use leftover ham)
- 6 slices Swiss cheese, cut into 4ths
- 6 TBSP butter, melted
- 2 TBSP Dijon mustard
- 1½ TBSP dried minced onion
- 2 tsp Worcestershire® sauce
- 1 tsp poppy seeds

Preheat oven to 350° F.

Cut ham and cheese slices to fit inside the rolls. Place two slices of ham and two slices of cheese 4ths on each roll. Place rolls on a lined baking sheet.

Melt butter in a small bowl in the microwave. Stir in mustard, minced onion, Worcestershire, and poppy seeds. Brush mixture over rolls with a pastry brush.

Cover loosely with aluminum foil. Bake 15 - 20 minutes. Serve immediately.

Lettuce

Attributes:

FEMININE,
MOON, WATER

Magical Properties:

CHASTITY, PROTECTION,
LOVE, SLEEP

Magical Uses:

Rub lettuce juice on your forehead or eat the leaves to help you fall asleep.
If you wish to preserve yourself against temptations of the flesh, eat lettuce.
Plant lettuce seeds in the form of the name of someone you love.
If the seeds sprout well, so too will love between you.

Veggie Subs

Yield: 6 - 12 Servings

- 1 pkg sub rolls
- Leaf lettuce, torn into bite-size pieces
- 2 Roma tomatoes, sliced
- ½ cucumber, peeled and sliced
- 1 green pepper, cut into strips
- 1 small onion, cut into rings, then cut in half
- 1 small can of sliced black olives
- Shredded sharp Cheddar cheese
- Mayonnaise
- Store-bought balsamic vinaigrette

Spread mayonnaise onto both sides of the sub roll. Add veggies, sprinkle on the desired amount of Cheddar cheese, and drizzle balsamic vinaigrette over the top.

Italian, Greek, and Olive oil vinaigrettes are all excellent substitutes. Add and change the veggies and cheese to your specific tastes. You can't get it wrong!

Figs

The energy of figs helps connect you to your intuition, making it easier to interpret the information you may otherwise not be aware of.

Cast a love spell by serving figs to your partner while you have a pink candle burning!

Attributes:

KNOWLEDGE, FERTILITY,
LUCK, LOVE,
PROTECTION

Fig & Prosciutto Flatbread

Yield: 2 Flatbreads

- 2 (4.4 ounces) Naan® Flatbread (1 package)
- 2 tsp extra virgin olive oil
- 1 garlic clove, minced
- ⅓ cup fig jam
- 4 oz brie cheese, thinly sliced
- 2 oz prosciutto, chopped
- ½ cup fresh baby arugula or leaf lettuce

Preheat oven to 350° F.

Combine the olive oil and minced garlic. Brush each piece of flatbread with the mixture.

Spread the fig jam evenly over the surface of each flatbread. Top off with the sliced brie and chopped prosciutto.

Bake for 15 minutes until the cheese has melted and the prosciutto is crispy. Remove from the oven and cut each flatbread into wedges.

Top with a sprinkling of fresh baby arugula or leaf lettuce. Serve immediately.

Sassafras

Use the chips of sassafras root bark to craft a bed, gate, or object to be free from the influence of malevolent spirits. Burn the wood chips as incense to rid a place of negative influence.

Make a wand from sassafras wood to free places, people, and objects from the sway of evil spirits. Its twisty nature lends it to this purpose.

Slow Cooker Pork BBQ

Yield: 8 - 10 Servings
Reheats well

- 2 lb pork tenderloin
- 12 oz can root beer (non-diet)
- Your favorite BBQ Sauce
- Martin's® Potato Sandwich rolls

Place pork in the slow cooker and pour in root beer. Cover and cook on low for 6 -7 hours.

Remove pork and shred with 2 forks. Place in a large mixing bowl.

Heat BBQ sauce in a medium pot over medium heat then stir into the shredded pork. Serve on Martin's® Potato Sandwich rolls.

Oats

Oats increase fortitude, endurance, persistence, personal change, meditation, faithfulness, good luck, comfort, spiritual growth, and achieving balance in your life.

Use oats when focusing on areas of happiness, health, tradition, stability, or family matters.

Apple Valley Sandwiches

- Multigrain sandwich bread, toasted
- Honey-mustard
- Romaine lettuce, torn into bite-size pieces
- Smoked turkey from the deli
- Smoked Mozzarella or Gouda cheese from the deli
- 1 sweet apple (such as Fuji or Gala) sliced thin

Toast bread slices lightly and let cool.

Spread honey-mustard on each slice of toast. Add the desired amount of lettuce and turkey, a slice of cheese, and apple slices to fit.

Make as many as you want.

Black Beans

Associations:

MERCURY,
AIR,
MASCULINE

Magical Properties:

CREATIVITY, COMMUNICATION,
OVERCOMING HURDLES, MAKING
DECISIONS, WISDOM, AND PROSPERITY

Southwest Chicken Tortilla Sandwiches

Yield: 8 Servings
Serve leftovers cold or at room temperature

- 3 boneless, skinless chicken breasts
- 1 bottle Heinz® Kansas City Style Sweet & Smokey® BBQ sauce
- ¼ cup Ranch dressing
- 1 can of Black beans, drained
- 1 can of corn, drained
- 2 cups chopped lettuce leaves
- 1 cup chopped onion
- 1 8-count package of large tortillas

Mix ¼ cup BBQ sauce and ¼ cup Ranch dressing in a small bowl. Cover and refrigerate for later.

Wash chicken and place in the slow cooker. Cover chicken with remaining BBQ sauce, cover, and cook on low for 5 - 6 hours. When chicken is done, shred with two forks.

Place drained black beans and corn in separate small bowls. Place chopped lettuce and onion in separate small bowls.

Lay tortilla flat on a plate. Using a spoon, lightly spread the BBQ/Ranch dressing mixture on the tortilla (like putting mayo on a sandwich) but stay about an inch from the edge.

Place a layer of lettuce down the center, layer a generous portion of the shredded chicken, next layer black beans, corn, and onions. Drizzle a bit more of the BBQ/Ranch sauce over the top, wrap from the sides and enjoy!

.

Red Leaf Lettuce

Dreaming of red leaf lettuce could represent your fear of loss.

Dreams of eating red leaf lettuce could indicate a joyous occasion.
However, it will be of short duration.

Apple and Goat Cheese Flatbread

Yield: 2 Servings

- 1 2-pack of Stonefire Naan Ancient Grains® (or original) flatbread (DO NOT USE THE GARLIC FLAVOR)
- 1 8-oz package of shredded Mozzarella cheese
- 1 Fuji apple, sliced thin
- 1 onion, sliced, rings separated
- 1½ oz walnut halves
- 2 tsp sugar
- ½ oz chopped red leaf lettuce (or your favorite lettuce)
- 1 oz goat cheese
- 2 TBSP balsamic vinegar
- 1 tsp honey
- 2 TBSP water

Preheat the oven to 400° F.

Line a baking sheet with aluminum foil. Place flatbreads on the baking sheet and sprinkle generously with Mozzarella to within an inch of the edges. Set aside.

Slice the onion; wash and slice the apple; chop and wash the lettuce; crumble the goat cheese; coarsely chop walnuts.

In a small ramekin or other small bowl, mix the balsamic vinegar and honey. Set aside.

In a small non-stick skillet, over medium-low heat, add 1 TBSP olive oil, 2 TBSP water, 2 tsp sugar, the onions, and walnuts, and stir constantly until onions are caramelized, the walnuts are shiny and sticky, and all water is evaporated. About 5 minutes. Set aside.

Place flatbreads in the oven for about 5 minutes or long enough for the cheese to melt. Remove from the oven and place the apple slices all the way around each flatbread. Sprinkle the onion-walnut mixture over each; then sprinkle each with the goat cheese crumbles; top the center of each with a handful of lettuce; drizzle the balsamic-honey mixture lightly over each flatbread.

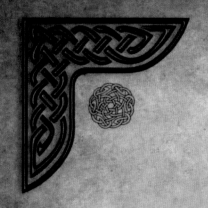

Entrees

Lemons

Associations:

MOON, WATER,
FEMININITY

Attributes:

LOVE, HAPPINESS
RENEWAL, SPIRITUALITY,
AND PURITY

Magical Properties:

To remove negative energy hang sachets of dried
lemon rinds in your closet. To encourage sleep, place
a few lemon leaves under your pillow. Add a few
drops of lemon oil to your laundry to draw new
friends into your life.

Tuscan Chicken Linguini

Yield: 4 Servings
Not the best reheated, but okay

- 1 lemon, cut into four wedges
- 3 Roma tomatoes, cut into wedges
- 1 TBSP Tuscan Heat Spice (recipe below)
- 12 oz Linguini
- 20 oz boneless, skinless chicken breasts, cut into stir-fry strips
- 6 TBSP cream cheese
- 2 TBSP Kerrygold® Garlic Herb butter
- ¾ cup Parmesan cheese
- ½ oz fresh basil leaves
- Olive oil
- Salt and pepper to taste
- 1 TBSP butter

Tuscan Heat Spice

- 4 tsp dried basil
- 2 tsp dried rosemary
- 2 tsp oregano
- 1 tsp cayenne pepper
- 1 tsp ground fennel

Blend Tuscan Heat Spice together in an empty spice jar or small air-tight container and label for future use.

Adjust oven rack to upper position and preheat oven to 400° F.

Bring a large pot of salted water to a boil.

Zest ½ tsp lemon rind, then cut lemon into quarters. Squeeze 1 TBSP juice into a small bowl and save the remaining lemon for another use. Cut tomato into ½ inch thick wedges.

Tuscan Chicken Linguini

Continued...

Pull basil leaves from stems and roughly chop or tear leaves.

Line a baking sheet with aluminum foil, then arrange tomato wedges on it, skin side down. Sprinkle with a drizzle of olive oil. Season with salt and pepper and 1 tsp Tuscan Heat Spice. Roast in oven until wilted and beginning to release their juices (about 25 minutes).

When the tomatoes have roasted for about 10 minutes, add linguini to boiling water. Cook 10 - 12 minutes, then drain, reserving ½ cup of pasta cooking water. Set aside in colander and keep pot handy for later use.

Pat washed chicken dry with paper towels and season with salt and pepper and enough Tuscan Heat Spice to coat. Heat a drizzle of olive oil in a large skillet over medium-high heat. Add chicken and cook, occasionally tossing, until browned and cooked through, 3 - 4 minutes. Remove from heat.

In the pot you cooked the pasta in, add 1 TBSP butter and melt over medium-high heat. Add lemon zest, cream cheese, and ⅓ cup pasta cooking water, and whisk until smooth. Stir in linguini, garlic-herb butter, reserved lemon juice, and half the Parmesan. If pasta seems dry, add more cooking water, a little at a time, until coated in a loose sauce. Toss in chicken, then season with salt and pepper to taste.

Plate pasta and top individual servings with tomato wedges, basil, and remaining Parmesan.

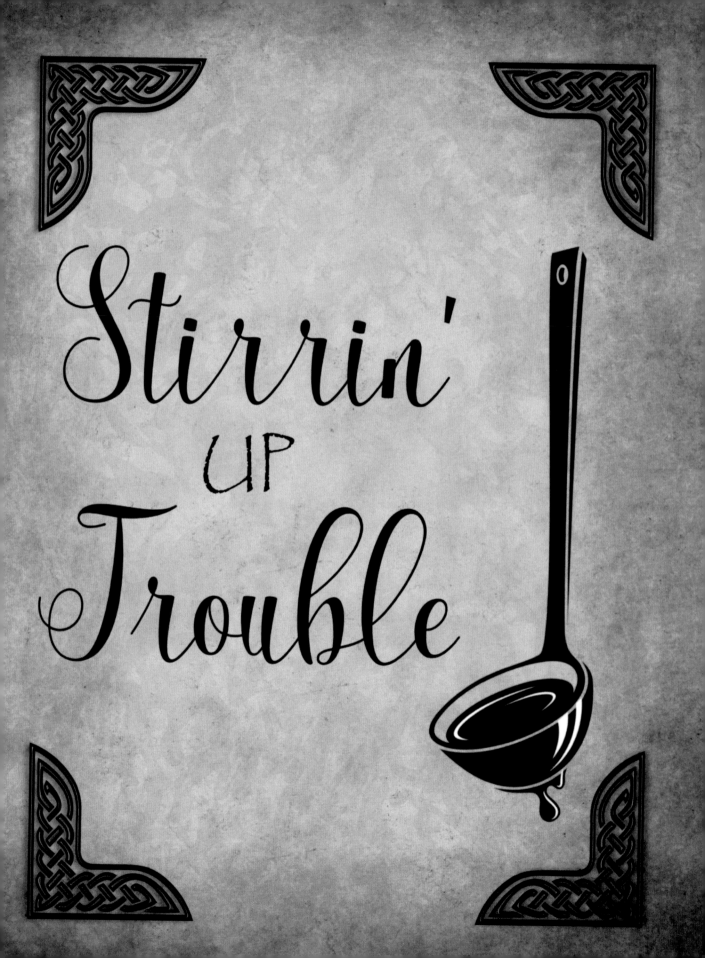

Red Bell Peppers

Dreaming about red bell pepper means you are feeling overwhelmed and burdened. There is an issue that you are avoiding.

Dreams about red bell peppers signify your inhibitions are hindering your creativity. You are afraid others will know of your shortcomings. You need to let loose and adopt a more carefree attitude.

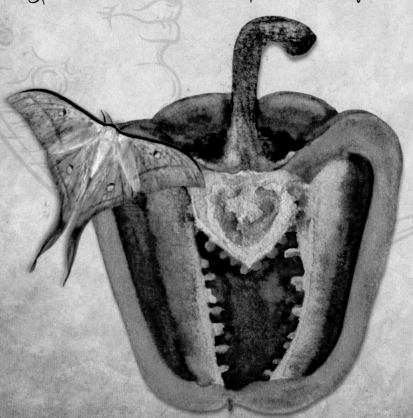

Chicken & Orzo Frittata

Yield: 2 - 4 Servings
Does not reheat well

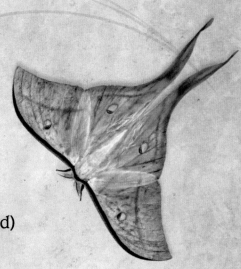

- 1 Rotisserie chicken, chopped
- ¾ cup orzo pasta, cooked
- ½ cup chopped onion
- ½ cup roasted red peppers, chopped
- 1 TBSP olive oil
- 6 eggs
- ½ cup chopped parsley (or 1 TBSP dried)
- ⅓ cup ricotta cheese
- 2 TBSP sour cream
- Salt and pepper to taste

Preheat oven to 400° F.

Slice red pepper into strips, then place in a Ziploc bag with olive oil. Toss to coat. Place on a lined baking sheet and place in an oven set at 400° F for 20 minutes. When cooled, chop and set aside.

Decrease oven temperature to 325° F.

Cook orzo according to package directions.

In a large mixing bowl, break the egg yolks with a whisk. Add ricotta, sour cream, parsley, and veggies.

Remove orzo, strain, and cool. Add chicken to the egg mixture, then add orzo.

Pour mixture into greased baking dish and bake at 325° F for 15 minutes, then broil for 5 minutes.

Candle Color Meanings

White:
SPIRITUALITY, PEACE, PURITY

Black:
BANISHING, PROTECTION, BINDING

Greene:
NATURE, HEALING, MONEY, FERTILITY

Yellow:
HOPE, INTELLIGENCE, COMFORT

Blue:
COMMUNICATION, TRAVELING, CALM

Red:
STRENGTH, PASSION, LUST

Creamy Italian Slow Cooker Chicken

Yield: 6 Servings
Reheats well

- 4 - 6 boneless, skinless chicken breasts
- ½ stick butter
- 4 oz cream cheese, softened
- 1 can cream of chicken soup
- 1 packet Italian Seasoning Dressing Mix

Wash chicken and place in the slow cooker.

Melt butter in the microwave and pour into a medium-size mixing bowl. Add cream cheese, chicken soup, and dressing mix. Stir until combined and pour over chicken. Cover and cook on low for 6 - 8 hours.

Serve with plenty of sauce on top. You can also shred this chicken with two forks, place it on a bed of rice and drizzle the sauce from the slow cooker over the top.

Broccoli

Washing broccoli in a kitchen sink in your dream foretells that happy family times are coming.

If you dream of eating broccoli, you are searching for fresh ideas.

Dreaming about broccoli is a symbol of spiritual nourishment. The dream may indicate the need for more positive interactions to fulfill your spiritual void or reinforce that your path provides the spiritual energy you need.

Chicken, Rice & Broccoli Casserole

Yield: 8 Servings
Reheats well

- 3 - 4 large boneless, skinless chicken breasts, cooked and cut into bite-size pieces
- 4 TBSP butter, melted
- Salt and pepper to taste
- 1 cup long-grain rice, cooked
- 1 cup chopped onion
- 1 pkg frozen, chopped broccoli
- 1 can cream of chicken soup
- 2 cups extra-sharp shredded Cheddar cheese, divided

Preheat the oven to 350° F.

Wash chicken and place in a large baking dish. Drizzle with melted butter, then sprinkle with salt and pepper to taste. Bake for 50 minutes.

While the chicken is baking, cook the rice and chop the onion. Place broccoli in a colander and thaw under cold running water, using your hands to break it up.

When the chicken is done, cut it into bite-size pieces.

In a large mixing bowl, stir all ingredients until well blended, reserving 1 cup of the shredded cheese, then pour into a large, greased baking dish. Top evenly with the remaining cheese.

Bake in a pre-heated oven for 30 - 40 minutes. The cheese on top should be lightly golden brown.

Vinegar

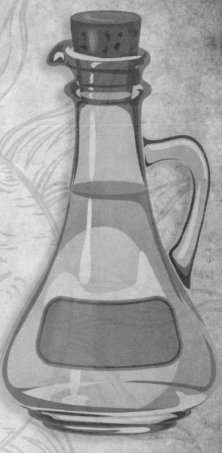

Associations:

Mars, Fire,
Masculine

Vinegar can be taken internally - one teaspoon a day
to protect against illness. You can also use it as a
gargle for sore throats.

Attributes:

Energy & Protection

Add a small amount of vinegar to your bath water for protection,
or sprinkle it around your boundary to create a circle of protection.

Mom's Overnight Baked or Grilled BBQ Chicken

Yield: 6 Servings
Reheats well

- 1½ - 2 lbs chicken (breasts, thighs, your cuts of choice)
- ½ cup white wine vinegar
- 4 TBSP Worcestershire® sauce
- ½ cup of water
- 1½ cup brown sugar
- 1½ cup ketchup
- 2 tsp salt
- 1½ tsp pepper
- 1½ tsp dry mustard
- 2 tsp paprika
- 2 dashes of Tabasco® sauce

Poach (boil) chicken for 30 minutes.

Combine all marinade ingredients, reserving 1 cup.

Place chicken in a large baking dish and pour marinade over the chicken. Cover with plastic wrap and refrigerate overnight. Refrigerate reserved marinade.

Grill chicken using the reserved marinade for basting, approximately 10 - 15 minutes per side, depending on your grill temperature. The internal chicken temperature should be 165° F when it's done.

This chicken can also be baked in a 350° F oven for 1 hour and it's almost as good as the grilled version.

Oranges

Drink a glass of orange juice before making a big decision
to help engage your intuition.

Think of a question as you eat your orange, then count the seeds.
An even number means no, and odd means yes.

Give oranges as gifts, either the fruit or as a flavoring in a dish or baked good,
to strengthen the bonds of friendship and give blessings and joy to the receiver.

Orange-Honey Sriracha Chicken

Yield: 4 Servings
Reheats well

- 4 boneless, skinless chicken breasts
- ½ cup orange juice
- ½ cup orange marmalade
- 2 TBSP lemon juice
- 2 TBSP Hoisin sauce
- 1 TBSP soy sauce
- 2 TBSP red wine vinegar
- 2 TBSP Sriracha sauce
- 1 tsp garlic powder
- 1 tsp salt
- ½ tsp ground ginger
- ¼ tsp ground black pepper

Preheat the oven to 350° F.

Wash chicken. Butter a medium baking dish.

Mix all ingredients together in a small mixing bowl. Pour half over the chicken and bake at 350° F for 1 hour.

Heat reserve sauce in a small saucepan and drizzle over plated chicken.

Witch's Kitchen Blessings

May all that be created here by means both magical and
mundane bring nourishment, healing, sustenance and
cause harm to none.

With love and peace, joy and magic, be now and always filled. So mote it be.

Parmesan Chicken Tenders with Garlic - Balsamic Dressing

Yield: 4 Servings
Reheats well

- 1 pkg chicken tenderloin (or 3 - 4 boneless, skinless chicken breasts)
- ½ cup buttermilk
- 1 cup Italian seasoned bread crumbs
- ½ cup fresh grated Parmesan cheese
- Olive oil for drizzling

Dressing
- 4 or 5 cloves garlic, minced
- 3 TBSP Balsamic vinegar
- ½ cup olive oil
- ½ tsp salt
- ½ tsp pepper

Preheat oven to 500° F.

Marinate chicken in buttermilk for 30 minutes in the refrigerator.

Combine Italian seasoned bread crumbs and Parmesan cheese in a medium size mixing bowl. Set aside.

Remove chicken from buttermilk marinade and dredge in breadcrumb mixture. Place in greased baking dish. Drizzle with a little olive oil and bake at 500° F for 12 minutes.

In a small bowl, add salt and pepper to minced garlic to form a paste. Add another dash of salt and pepper and stir in Balsamic vinegar and olive oil. Drizzle over plated chicken.

Tabasco Sauce

Dreaming about hot sauce could mean you desire to be saucier with your partner in order to spice up your love life.

You may be trying to attract someone who isn't getting the message, and you need to be bolder and more direct.

Slow cooker Honey Mustard Chicken

Yield: 4 Servings

- 4 chicken breasts
- 1 tsp Tabasco®
- 3 cloves of garlic, minced
- ½ cup honey
- ¼ cup whole-grain mustard
- ¼ cup Dijon mustard
- 2 TBSP water
- 2 TBSP cornstarch

In a small bowl, mix together the Tabasco, garlic, honey, Dijon, and whole-grain mustard.

Place chicken breasts in the slow cooker and pour the honey mustard sauce over the top. Cover and cook for 6 hours on low.

When the chicken is done, mix the cornstarch and water in a small bowl until it forms a paste.

Remove the chicken breasts from the slow cooker and stir the cornstarch mixture into the cooking liquid. Return the chicken breasts to the slow cooker. Cook on high for 15 - 30 minutes or until the sauce has thickened.

Serve with sauce drizzled over the top of the chicken.

Hoisin Sauce

A dream about hoisin sauce means that you are worried about making mistakes or you are trying to hide your mistakes or failures.

But if you dream of eating food in hoisin sauce, it is a good omen, indicating family harmony and a happy life.

Easy Mongolian Beef Noodles

Yield: 6 Servings
Reheats well

- 1 lb lean ground beef
- 4 tsp minced ginger
- 6 cloves garlic, minced
- ½ cup low sodium soy sauce
- ½ cup of Kitchen Basics® Beef Stock
- 2 TBSP Knorr® Beef Concentrate Stock
- ¼ cup brown sugar
- 6 TBSP hoisin sauce
- ½ tsp red pepper flakes
- ½ tsp black pepper
- 1 lb box of linguine noodles
- 4 green onions, diced for garnish
- Toasted sesame seeds for garnish

In a large, deep skillet, brown the ground beef over medium heat. Drain fat and return to skillet. Stir in the ginger and garlic and cook another 2 - 3 minutes.

While the ground beef is cooking, get a pot of water started for your pasta noodles. Be sure to salt the water well so that your noodles soak up that flavor.

Combine the remaining ingredients—soy sauce, beef broth, Knorr® Beef Concentrate, brown sugar, red pepper flakes, pepper, and hoisin sauce in a small mixing bowl and pour into the ground beef mixture. Let simmer in the pan for about 3 minutes to allow the ground beef to absorb the flavors.

Once your pasta is done cooking, transfer the noodles to the ground beef mixture. Mix thoroughly and allow to cook for another minute or two to allow the sauce to thicken.

Top each plated serving with green onions and toasted sesame seeds.

NOTE: This is a spicy dish. Half the black pepper and red pepper flakes for a less spicy dish.

Gnocchi

Dreaming about gnocchi means you are busy with important matters.
You have a lot of energy and drive to get ahead.

Dreams reflect an opportunity that you have yet to seize.
You have a prosperous prospect at your fingertips.

Cheeseburger Gnocchi

Yield: 6 Servings

- 1 TBSP butter
- 1 16 oz package potato gnocchi
- ½ lb lean ground beef
- 1 tsp salt
- 1 tsp pepper
- ½ tsp smoked paprika
- 1 tsp cumin
- 1 tsp mustard powder
- 2 cups diced onion (about 1 whole onion. 1½ cups in prep, ½ cup for topping)
- 3 - 4 cloves garlic, minced
- 1 10-oz can Ro-Tel® Diced Tomatoes and Green Chiles
- 1 cup beef broth or stock
- ¼ cup heavy cream
- 1 cup shredded sharp Cheddar cheese (½ in prep, ½ for topping)
- ⅓ cup thinly sliced green onions

Melt butter in a 12-inch skillet over medium-high heat. Add gnocchi in a single layer and cook on one side for 2 - 3 minutes until browned and toasted. Shake the pan to toss the gnocchi and continue cooking for another 2 - 3 minutes, tossing occasionally, until both sides are toasted. Place gnocchi on a plate and set it aside.

Turn the heat to high and return the skillet to the stove. When the pan is very hot and smoking, add the ground beef and season with salt, pepper, cumin, paprika, and mustard powder. Add the onion and garlic, and cook, stirring occasionally, until the beef is browned and the onions are golden. Drain off fat if necessary.

Add the tomatoes, broth, and gnocchi back into the skillet. Stir to combine. Bring to a boil, then cover, reduce heat to medium-low, and simmer for 5 minutes until the gnocchi is tender and the liquid is mostly absorbed.

Remove from heat, then add the cream and ½ cup of shredded Cheddar cheese and stir to combine. Top with remaining cheese and green onions. Place the skillet under the broiler in the oven until cheese is browned and bubbly, about 3 minutes.

Beltane

This Wiccan holiday is celebrated on May 1st, or May Day, recognizing spring at its peak and the coming summer. This holiday is associated very strongly with fertility.

This festival originated in Ireland and is often commemorated with bonfires. maypoles, dancing, and performing fertility rituals. Beltane is a Celtic word and referred to the Celtic sun god, Belenus. The Celts used to light two bonfires because they believed it would purify themselves and increase their fertility.

Savory Slow Cooker London Broil

Yield: 6 Servings
Reheats well

- 1½ - 2 lbs London Broil
- 1 tsp black pepper
- 1 packet Lipton® Onion Soup Mix
- 1 small onion cut into wedges
- 1½ cups Kitchen Basics® Beef Stock

Place London Broil in the slow cooker. Add beef stock. Sprinkle beef with pepper and Lipton® Onion Soup Mix. Cover and cook on low for 6 - 8 hours.

Remove from slow cooker, slice thin and serve.

Mushrooms

Associations:
LONGEVITY, STRENGTH

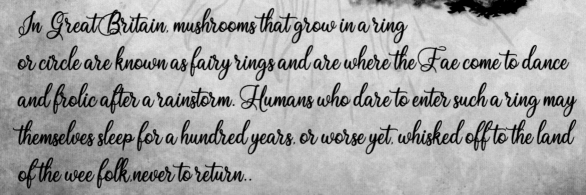

In Great Britain, mushrooms that grow in a ring
or circle are known as fairy rings and are where the Fae come to dance
and frolic after a rainstorm. Humans who dare to enter such a ring may
themselves sleep for a hundred years, or worse yet, whisked off to the land
of the wee folk, never to return..

Simple Slow Cooker London Broil

Yield: 6 Servings
Reheats well

- 1½ - 2 lbs London Broil
- 1¼ cup Kitchen Basics® Beef Stock
- 2 cloves garlic, minced
- 4 - 5 slices of onion, cut into halves, rings separated
- 1 small can of mushrooms, drained
- 1 cup of red wine
- ½ tsp black pepper
- ¼ tsp dried thyme
- 2 tsp water
- 2 tsp cornstarch
- 1 - 2 cups cooked rice or egg noodles

Place London Broil in the slow cooker and sprinkle with black pepper. Add garlic, onions, beef stock, and red wine. Cover and cook on low for 6 hours, adding mushrooms in the last hour of cooking.

Remove meat and slice thin. Set aside and keep warm.

Mix water and cornstarch to create a paste. Transfer cooking liquid from slow cooker to small saucepan. Over medium heat, slowly stir in cornstarch mixture and constantly stir until sauce thickens.

Serve meat over cooked rice or egg noodles and drizzle sauce over plated beef.

Soy Beans

Associations:

Spirituality,
Good Health, Virtuous

Dreaming of soybeans indicates health, happiness, a sweeter relationship with your partner, and a life that is rich. You are determined to create your own career.

Slow Cooked Pepper Steak

Yield: 4 Servings
Reheats well

- 1½ - 2 lbs London Broil or beef round steak
- 2 TBSP canola oil
- ¼ cup low sodium soy sauce
- 1 clove of garlic, minced
- 1 cup onion, chopped
- 2 large green peppers, cut into strips
- 4 medium tomatoes, cut into eight wedges
- 1 tsp sugar
- ½ tsp salt
- ¼ tsp pepper
- ¼ tsp ground ginger
- 1 - 2 cups cooked rice

Heat canola oil over medium-high heat in a large skillet. Brown the beef on both sides, approximately 4 minutes per side. Transfer beef to slow cooker.

Combine soy sauce, garlic, onions, sugar, salt, pepper and ginger. Pour over meat. Cover and cook on low for 5 hours.

Add green peppers and tomatoes to the slow cooker and cook for an additional hour.

Serve over cooked rice.

Salt

Salt is a powerful tool and can be used to cast a circle to create a powerful barrier that shields and protects while working magic, a time when a witch is at their most powerful or most vulnerable.

Salt is used in banishing, binding, cleansing, healing, purification and protection, as well as blessings and consecrations. Salt may be used to represent the element of earth on an altar.

Italian Herb Baked Meatballs

Yield: 6 - 8 Servings or approximately 30 meatballs
Reheats well

- 1 lb ground beef
- ½ cup Panko® breadcrumbs
- ½ cup freshly grated Parmesan cheese
- ½ cup onion, diced
- 2 TBSP skim milk
- 2 cloves garlic, minced
- 1 egg, lightly beaten
- 2 TBSP Pampered Chef® Rosemary Herb Seasoning
- 1 TBSP oregano
- ½ tsp Kosher salt
- ½ tsp black pepper
- Olive oil

Preheat the oven to 375° F. Line a baking sheet with parchment paper or non-stick aluminum foil.

In a large mixing bowl, combine all ingredients and mix with your hands (like you're making a meatloaf) until well blended.

Wash your hands, then oil the palms of your hands with olive oil and form 1-inch meatballs placing each on the baking sheet. The olive oil on your hands prevents the meat from sticking to your hands and keeps the meat moist. Keep the meatballs close in size so they cook evenly.

Bake for 20 - 22 minutes or until the meatballs are lightly browned and cooked through.

No sauce required! Delicious on their own, or you can add a favorite tomato sauce or gravy.

Sesame Oil

Sesame seeds are said to have the power to open locks, reveal hidden passages or find hidden treasures. They also are used in magic to induce lust.

When going for a job interview, decide what salary You want, then touch a little sesame oil on the pulse spots on your wrists. Be confident in asking for the required sum.

Slow Cooker Mongolian Beef

Yield: 6 Servings
Reheats well

- 1½ - 2 lbs London Broil
- ¼ cup cornstarch
- 1 TBSP toasted Sesame oil
- 2 cloves garlic, minced
- 1 tsp ginger root, minced
- ½ cup low sodium soy sauce
- ⅓ cup brown sugar
- ½ cup of water
- ½ cup sliced green onions
- 2 cups cooked rice

Coat London Broil with cornstarch and place in the slow cooker.

In a small mixing bowl, stir together all remaining ingredients except green onions.

Pour over beef, cover, and cook on low for 6 - 8 hours.

Cook rice according to package directions about 20 minutes before beef is done.

Slice or shred beef, serve over rice, and top with sliced green onions. Drizzle cooking liquids from the slow cooker over the top.

Rosemary

Attributes:

Memory, Loyalty, Protection, Purification, and Healing

Associations:

Fire, Sun, Masculine, Leo, Scorpio

Burn dried rosemary leaves to cleanse and purify a space. Plant rosemary to ward off negativity. To boost your memory, drink rosemary tea or use rosemary oil in a diffuser.

Pork Loin with Wine and Herb Gravy

Yield: 6 Servings
Reheats well

- 2 lbs boneless, center cut pork loin
- 5 cloves of garlic, minced
- 1 tsp ground sage
- 2 tsp Pampered Chef® Rosemary Herb Seasoning
- 1 cup Kitchen Basics® Chicken Stock
- ½ tsp Kosher salt
- ½ tsp black pepper
- ½ cup white or blush wine
- ¼ cup heavy cream
- 2 tsp cornstarch
- 2 tsp water

Place pork in the slow cooker and pour in chicken stock. Place minced garlic in chicken stock around the pork. Sprinkle with Kosher salt and black pepper, then sprinkle with sage and Rosemary Herb Seasoning. Cover and cook on low for 6 - 8 hours.

Remove pork from slow cooker and slice on cutting board. Cover to keep warm.

Strain the cooking liquid in the slow cooker over a medium bowl. Place ¼ cup of the cooking liquid in a small saucepan. Over low-medium heat, stir in wine and heavy cream. Add a pinch of Kosher salt and black pepper and a pinch of sage and Rosemary Herb Seasoning. If the sauce doesn't thicken on its own, mix 2 tsp of water with 2 tsp of cornstarch and slowly stir in, cooking another 2 - 3 minutes or until gravy thickens. Gravy should be thickened slightly, not super thick.

Drizzle gravy over plated pork.

Raspberries

Associations:

FEMALE, WATER,
MOON, VENUS, PISCES

Raspberries are thought to invoke fertility and can be used in wine to create a simple love potion. Use dried berries and leaves in the bath to keep your partner at home and carry with you to bring luck in your marriage.

Planting a raspberry bush near the home or business can protect it.

Pork Roast in Raspberry Chipotle Sauce

Yield: 6 - 8 Servings
Reheats well

- 1 small onion, sliced and separated into rings
- 3 lbs pork loin roast
- 1 (8 oz) jar of seedless raspberry preserves
- ⅓ cup apple juice
- 1 can chipotle peppers in adobo sauce
- 2 TBSP Balsamic vinegar

Place onions on the bottom of the slow cooker. Place pork on top of onions.

Using a blender or electric mixer combine preserves, 2 chipotle peppers, apple juice, and balsamic vinegar. Blend until smooth. Pour over pork.

Cover and cook on low for 8 hours.

Sage

Attributes:

Luck, Wisdom,
Purification,
Prosperity

Associations:

Air, Masculinity,
Gemini, Sagittarius,
and Pisces

Carry sage leaves with you for wisdom and to connect to your intuition. Smoke cleanse your home with a sage smudge stick to raise the positive vibrations. Plant sage in your garden to attract success and abundance.

Slow Cooked Brown Sugar Glazed Pork Loin

Yield: 6 Servings
Reheats well

- 2 lbs pork loin roast
- 1 clove of garlic, minced
- 1 tsp ground sage
- ¼ tsp pepper
- ½ tsp salt
- 1 TBSP Balsamic vinegar
- 1 TBSP olive oil
- 1 cup of water
- 1 TBSP soy sauce
- ¼ cup Balsamic vinegar
- ½ cup brown sugar
- 2 TBSP water
- 2 TBSP cornstarch

In small bowl mix garlic, sage, salt, and pepper. Rub over pork and place in the slow cooker.

In another small bowl mix 1 TBSP Balsamic vinegar, 1 TBSP olive oil, and 1 cup of water. Pour into the slow cooker without pouring over the pork. Cover and cook on low for 6 - 8 hours.

Just before the pork is ready, in a small saucepan, over medium heat, combine the remaining balsamic vinegar, soy sauce, and brown sugar. While that is heating, mix 2 TBSP water with 2 TBSP cornstarch to form a paste. When the sauce is heated, slowly stir in the cornstarch mixture, stirring constantly, until the sauce thickens to a glaze. Set aside and keep warm.

Remove pork from the slow cooker and slice. Drizzle brown sugar glaze over plated pork.

Water

Water charged under the moon is considered sacred and is associated with feminine energies and intuition.

Seasonal Rains: Water collected on the day or night of a solstice or equinox makes them rare.

Spring: New Ventures
Summer: Growth
Autumn: Gratitude
Winter: Blessing

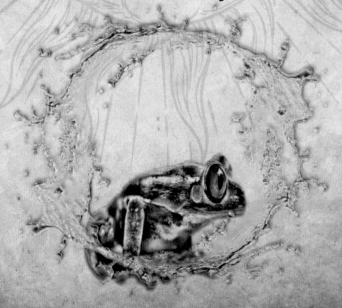

Brown Beans & Sausage

Yield: 8 Servings
Reheats well

- 1 small bag of dried pinto beans
- 1 pkg Eckrich® Turkey Smoked Skinless Sausage, sliced into ¼ inch discs
- 1 small onion, chopped
- 1 pkg Lipton® Onion Soup Mix
- ½ tsp pepper
- 6 - 8 cups of water
- 2 tsp olive oil

Place beans in a soup pot with enough water to cover beans by about 2 inches. Boil 5 minutes. Remove from heat, cover, and let soak for 1 hour.

Drain and rinse beans in a colander.

Using the same pot, sauté onions and sausage in olive oil until sausage starts to brown. Stir in beans; add 6 cups water, Lipton® Onion Soup mix, and pepper.

Bring to a boil, reduce heat to low, cover, and simmer for 2 - 3 hours until beans are soft. You'll have to judge the water quantity as it cooks as beans absorb a lot of liquid. Consistency should be like a thick stew so add water as necessary.

Maple Syrup

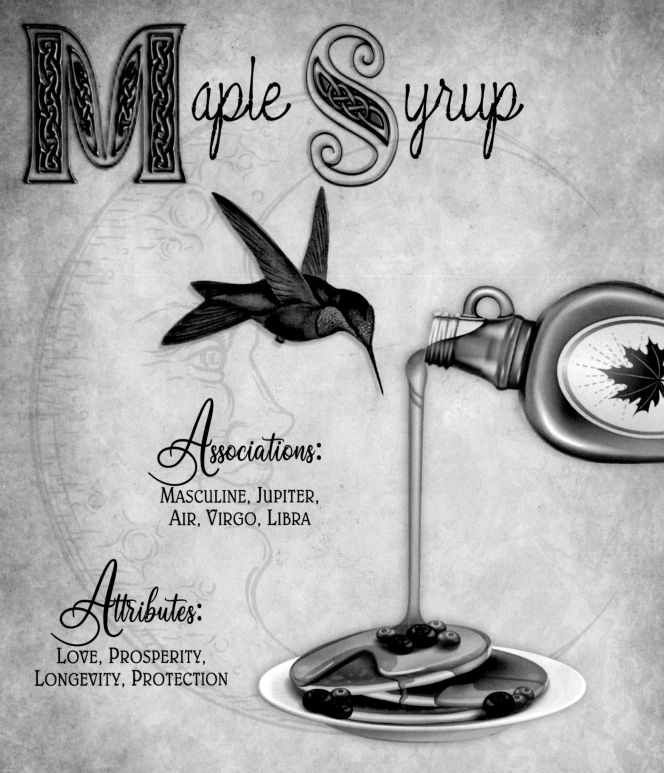

Associations:

Masculine, Jupiter,
Air, Virgo, Libra

Attributes:

Love, Prosperity,
Longevity, Protection

Maple wood is excellent for making wands.
Add maple syrup to food to attract money, and for long life.

Maple Mustard Glazed Salmon

Yield: 2 - 4 Servings
Does not reheat well

- 2 - 4 6 oz portions of salmon
- ¼ cup melted butter
- ½ cup maple syrup
- 2 TBSP spicy brown mustard
- 2 TBSP soy sauce
- ¼ tsp pepper

Preheat the oven to 425° F.

Arrange salmon in buttered baking dish. In a small bowl whisk all remaining ingredients and pour over the salmon.

Bake 15 - 20 minutes. Drizzle a bit of sauce over the salmon after plated.

.

Brown Sugar

Attributes:

Sweetness, Comfort, Love, Overcoming Enemies, and Making Them Your Friends

Dreaming about brown sugar indicates a passion and zest for life. Time to experiment and try new things, pushing beyond your limits. Your dream indicates harmony amongst friends and loved ones. You are broadening your mind and opening yourself to new experiences.

Sweet & Spicy Salmon

Yield: 2 - 4 Servings
Does not reheat well

- 2 - 4 6 oz salmon portions
- 5 TBSP brown sugar
- 1 tsp black pepper
- ½ tsp cayenne pepper
- 1 tsp dried minced onion
- ½ tsp paprika
- 1 clove of garlic, minced
- 4 TBSP Kikkoman® Low Sodium Soy Sauce
- 2 TBSP apple juice or orange juice

Preheat oven to 400° F.

Place salmon in a buttered baking dish.

Mix all ingredients together in a small mixing bowl and pour over the salmon.

Bake for 30 - 35 minutes. Drizzle a little sauce from the baking dish over each portion after plated.

Red Potatoes

Dreaming about red potatoes means you feel confident and self-assured. You are broadening your mind and opening yourself to new experiences.

While peeling or cooking red potatoes, imagine yourself safe and secure. Solidify your spell by envisioning yourself shrouded in a protective light that follows you wherever you go.

Rosemary Tilapia with Red Potatoes

Yield: 2 - 4 Servings
Does not reheat well

- 2 - 4 tilapia fillets
- 2 - 3 small red potatoes
- 1¼ tsp rosemary
- Salt and pepper to taste
- 2 TBSP butter, melted
- 2 TBSP olive oil

Preheat oven to 375° F.

Over a large cutting board, salt and pepper tilapia on both sides. Set aside.

On a separate cutting board, slice potatoes into thin round discs.

Layer potato slices on top of the fish from end to end, overlapping the potatoes just a little on each edge.

Melt 1 TBSP butter in a small bowl in the microwave, then stir in 1 TBSP olive oil.

Sprinkle salt and pepper over the layered potatoes and top with rosemary, then drizzle with the butter and olive oil mixture.

Combine remaining butter and olive oil in a large oven-safe skillet and heat on the stovetop to fairly high heat. Put fillets in the pan, potato side down, for 1 minute. Remove from the stovetop and place in the oven for 15 - 17 minutes.

.

Fish

The spiritual message of dreaming about fish in water is to pay attention to your spiritual life, which will give you clarity as to what is pouring over into your physical life.

In the Tarot, the symbol of a fish appears on all of the cup cards in the Royal Arcana. Cups are related to the element of water and represent feelings, emotions, and intuition. The royal arcana represents our self-governance and beliefs. It shows how we make decisions, and who or what those decisions are based on.

Simple Baked Turbot Fillet

Yield: 2 Servings
Does not reheat well

- 12 - 16 oz turbot fillet, or other light, flaky white fish
- 4 TBSP butter, melted
- ¼ tsp lemon juice
- 1 tsp garlic powder
- 1 tsp Penzey's® Cajun Seasoning
- Salt and pepper to taste
- Olive oil-flavored cooking spray

Preheat oven to 425° F.

Salt and pepper both sides of the fish and place in a baking dish sprayed with olive oil-flavored cooking spray.

Melt butter in a small bowl in the microwave. Stir in lemon juice and drizzle over fish.

Sprinkle garlic powder over the fish, then sprinkle Cajun seasoning over the fish. Bake 25 - 30 minutes. Fish should not be wet looking, but moist and flaky. It should be separating on the top when it's done.

Almonds

Almonds are used in prosperity and money spells. Additionally, climbing an almond tree is said to ensure success in business ventures.

Magical wands are made of almond wood, for it is a plant affiliated with Air, which is the elemental ruler of the magic wand. Placing almonds in your pocket will lead you to treasures.

Affiliations:

MASCULINE,
MERCURY,
AIR

Shrimp and Green Bean Salad over Smoked Gouda Grits

Yield: 6 Servings
Does not reheat well

- 1 lb peeled raw shrimp
- ¾ cup basil vinaigrette
- 6 cooked bacon strips, crumbled
- ½ lb green beans, trimmed
- ¾ cup sliced almonds
- 2 cups instant grits
- Water
- Olive oil
- 1 tsp salt
- ½ tsp pepper
- 1⅓ cups smoked Gouda cheese, shredded or crumbled

Combine raw shrimp and ¾ cup of basil vinaigrette in a large Ziploc® bag. Seal and chill in the refrigerator for 15 minutes.

Boil green beans in salted water, reduce to simmer, and cover. Cook until crisp-tender. Drain and place in a large mixing bowl. It's okay for them to cool down.

Cook bacon, and crumble when cooled. Add to mixing bowl with green beans and toss in the sliced almonds.

Cook 2 cups of instant grits according to package directions. When all water is absorbed, stir in salt, pepper, and smoked Gouda cheese. Set aside and keep warm.

Remove shrimp from marinade and sauté in olive oil in a large skillet over medium to medium-high heat. Add enough water to cover the bottom of the skillet, creating a sauté-boil. Stir and turn shrimp constantly for 3 - 4 minutes until pink.

Toss shrimp with green bean mixture and serve over warm grits.

Know Your Broom (Besom)

Used during rituals to purify a space and sweep negative or residual energy away.

Placed at the entrance of a home to guard against negative or unwanted energies. Represents the element of water and sweeps away energetic clutter.

Grandma's Salmon Cakes

Yield: 6 Servings
Reheats well

- 1 large can (or 2 small) Double-Q® Pink Salmon (de-boned & skinned)
- ½ cup chopped onion
- ½ cup Bisquick®
- 1 egg
- 1 TBSP yellow mustard
- ¼ tsp celery salt
- ¼ tsp pepper
- 2 TBSP olive oil (divided)

Mix all ingredients together in a medium mixing bowl, reserving 1 TBSP olive oil. Form into patties (approximately 6) and place on cutting board.

Heat remaining olive oil in a skillet over medium heat. Sauté salmon cakes 3 - 4 minutes per side. They should be a little crispy on the outside.

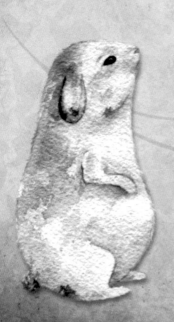

White Wine

Associations:

Joy, Happiness, Love, Relationships, Friendships, Endings, Success, Energy, Purification

Attributes:

Air, Summer

Pan Seared Scallops

Yield: 6 Servings
Does not reheat well

- 1 lb sea scallops
- 3 TBSP butter
- 1 TBSP olive oil
- 2 TBSP shallots, finely chopped
- 2 cloves garlic, minced
- ¼ cup white or blush wine
- ½ tsp lemon juice
- ½ tsp black pepper
- 1 tsp Penzey's® Cajun seasoning

In a large non-stick skillet heat 2 TBSPs butter and olive oil until almost smoking. Place each scallop in the pan and don't move them for 2 minutes. They must remain in place for browning. Adjust heat if necessary as you don't want them to burn. Turn each scallop over and leave it in place for 2 more minutes. You will know they're done when the slightly off-white center turns white. Once cooked, remove it from the pan and set it aside on a plate.

Add another TBSP of butter to the skillet and add the shallots and garlic and cook for one minute. Add wine and lemon. Cook another minute and add scallops back to the skillet, sprinkle with pepper and Cajun seasoning, and cook another minute until reheated. Do not cook longer than one minute or they will be overdone and rubbery.

Remove from pan and serve with pan sauce.

Zucchini

Zucchini are ruled by Jupiter. To stop a man from cheating, carve his name in the zucchini and freeze it. Eat zucchini cooked for protection and prosperity.

Dreaming about zucchini signifies glory, fame, prestige, wealth, abundance, victory, success, and healing. To see fried zucchini in your dream means that you will regain something you lost.

Shrimp and Zucchini Ribbons

Yield: 4 Servings
Does not reheat well

- 4 green onions, sliced, separating green from white
- 1 cup Jasmine rice
- 1 lemon cut into quarters
- 1 zucchini shaved into ribbons (using a vegetable peeler)
- 10 tsp basil-infused olive oil
- 1 TBSP plain olive oil
- 20 oz frozen or fresh shrimp, peeled
- 1 tsp chili flakes
- 4 TBSP butter, divided
- Salt and pepper to taste

Trim and thinly slice green onions, separating the greens and whites. Melt 1 TBSP butter in a small pot over medium-high heat. Add green onion whites and cook until just softened. Season with salt, pour in 1½ cups water, and bring to a boil. Add rice and stir to combine. Cover and cook until all water is absorbed.

Zest 1 tsp lemon rind, then cut the lemon into quarters. Trim ends from zucchini. Working over a large bowl, shave zucchini lengthwise into thin ribbons using a vegetable peeler, rotating as you go. Stop once you get to the seedy core.

Toss zucchini ribbons with basil-infused olive oil, half the lemon zest, season with salt and pepper, and squeeze in the juice from 2 lemon quarters. Set aside.

Rinse shrimp and pat dry with a paper towel. Season with salt and pepper.

Heat 1 TBSP plain olive oil and 1 TBSP butter in a large skillet over medium-high heat (use a non-stick pan if you have one). Add shrimp and season with chili flakes to taste–start with ¼ tsp and add more from there. Cook, tossing until pink and firm, about 3 - 5 minutes. While the shrimp cooks, place another 2 TBSP of butter in a small microwave-safe bowl and melt in the microwave. Squeeze in the juice from another lemon quarter. Stir and season with salt and pepper if desired.

Fluff rice with a fork and season with salt and pepper if desired. Divide between serving bowls. Shake off any excess marinade from the zucchini, then arrange ribbons on top of the rice. Place shrimp on top, drizzle with lemon butter, garnish with green onions, remaining lemon zest, and additional chili flakes to taste.

Salmon

Salmon symbolizes abundance, fertility, prosperity, and renewal.

Seeing a salmon swimming toward you in a dream symbolizes growing awareness and wisdom, and even a little luck. Your life brings fulfillment, even when things seem dire. Salmon leaping in your dream means that a new opportunity is approaching.

Sweet and Spicy Orange Salmon

Yield: 4 Servings
Does not reheat well

- Juice from one orange; about 1/4 cup
- Zest from one orange
- ¼ cup reduced-sodium soy sauce
- ¼ cup honey
- 1 tsp sesame oil
- 3 TBSP sriracha; more or less to taste
- 1½ - 2 lbs salmon fillets

Whisk together orange juice, orange zest, soy sauce, honey, sesame oil, and sriracha in a bowl. Reserve about ¼ cup of the sauce in a separate bowl for glazing later on.

Add the remaining sauce to a shallow dish and place the salmon in it to marinate for about 20 minutes, flipping the salmon over halfway through.

As the salmon is marinating, preheat oven to 400° F. You'll want a rack to be situated in the middle of the oven, as well as one near the top.

Line a baking sheet with foil and spray it with cooking spray.

Once the salmon has finished marinating, place the salmon on the prepared sheet, skin side down, and bake on the middle rack for about 18 minutes.

After 18 minutes, remove the sheet from the oven and brush the reserved ¼ cup of sauce over the salmon fillets.

Switch oven from bake to broil and place the sheet on the upper oven rack.

Broil for about 2 minutes or until the edges of the salmon begin to crisp and brown.

Limes

Attributes:

GROWTH, ABUNDANCE, AND MONEY

Limes are often used in love spells, but where oranges and lemons attract a lover, limes are used to keep them faithful to you. They can also be used to drive someone away or sour a relationship between two people.

Use limes to cleanse negative energy from a space or to get rid of bad luck and attract good fortune in its place.

Orange-Soy Glazed Scallops

Yield: 3 - 4 Servings
Does not reheat well

- ½ cup fresh orange juice (about 4 oranges), plus the zest from one orange
- ¼ cup low-sodium soy sauce
- 1 TBSP fresh lime juice (1 lime)
- 4 cloves garlic, minced
- 1 lb sea scallops
- 1 TBSP unsalted butter
- 1 TBSP olive oil
- Kosher salt to taste
- Feshly ground black pepper, to taste
- 1 green onion, green part only, thinly sliced

In a small saucepan over medium-high heat, combine the orange juice, soy sauce, lime juice, and garlic. Bring to a simmer and reduce until thickened into a syrup, about 10 minutes. (Be careful not to over-reduce the sauce).

If not already done, remove the small muscle or 'foot' from the scallops. Just pinch it between your thumb and first finger, and tear it away. Rinse under cool water and thoroughly pat dry.

Add the butter and olive oil to a large sauté pan over high heat. Season both sides of the scallops with salt and pepper, and once the pan lets off the first wisp of smoke, gently add the scallops to the pan, making sure they don't touch. Sear the scallops for 1½ minutes on each side.

To serve, place a dollop of the orange-soy glaze on a plate (one for each scallop) and place a scallop on top. Garnish with a little orange zest and a couple of scallion slices. Serve immediately. Enjoy!

Butternut Squash

Butternut Squash is related to pumpkin, so you get the associations with Samhain/Halloween. Protection, divination, banishing, and prosperity.

Attributes:

FERTILITY, ABUNDANCE, LOVE, PROSPERITY, AND GOOD LUCK

Creamy Orzo Pasta with Roasted Butternut Squash

Yield: 4 Servings
Reheats well

- 2 TBSP olive oil (will be added 1 TBSP at a time)
- 1 large butternut squash, approximately 2 lbs. (frozen, cubed butternut squash works just as well)
- Salt and pepper to taste
- 2 shallots
- 2 - 3 cloves of garlic
- 1 tsp dried sage (will be added ½ tsp at a time)
- 2½ cups orzo
- 5 cups vegetable stock (plus 1/2 cup if needed)
- 1 cup kale, chopped
- ¾ cup freshly grated Parmesan cheese

Preheat the oven to 400° F.

Peel, de-seed, and cut butternut squash into bite-sized cubes, season with salt, pepper, and 1 TBSP of olive oil. Arrange on a baking sheet and sprinkle with ½ tsp sage. Roast at 400° F for 45 minutes or until golden.

20 minutes before the squash is done, heat 1 TBSP of olive oil in a deep pan and sauté chopped shallots, garlic, and the other ½ tsp sage over low heat for 2 - 3 minutes.

Add vegetable stock, salt, and kale, and bring to a boil. Add orzo and cook for approximately 8 -10 minutes until orzo is tender. Stir throughout the cooking process to release starch and to avoid it sticking to the bottom of the pan. If the mixture looks too thick, add the additional ½ cup of vegetable stock or water to maintain creamy, risotto-like consistency. Remove from heat and stir in Parmesan cheese, salt to taste, and top with roasted butternut squash.

Parmesan Cheese

To dream of Parmesan cheese suggests success is coming, but not without effort: try to be patient and keep calm at all times.

New businesses, ventures, and investments with other people arrive. Dreaming of cheese means extreme optimism, but don't act on emotions. Analyze and plan your decisions.

Cacio e Pepe
(Italian for Cheese and Pepper)

Yield: 4 Servings
Reheats well

- 2 TBSP butter
- 2 TBSP extra virgin olive oil
- 2 tsp freshly ground pepper
- Kosher salt
- 1 lb spaghetti or other long pasta
- 2 cups freshly grated Parmesan cheese, plus more for serving / topping

Bring a large pot of water to a boil. While waiting for the water to boil, combine butter, olive oil, and pepper in a large skillet over medium-low heat, so the butter melts and the pepper becomes fragrant, about 2 minutes. Remove from heat and set aside.

Once water is boiling, add a generous amount of salt (about 2 TBSP), and then add the pasta, cooking until al dente, about 8 - 9 minutes. Remove from heat.

Add ½ cup of pasta water to the skillet with the melted butter and olive oil. Using tongs, quickly add the pasta directly from the pot and toss well to coat thoroughly. Add the cheese, and continue to toss pasta well, adding a bit more pasta water (1 - 2 TBSP) to achieve a creamy consistency. Season to taste with salt and more pepper if desired. Portion into bowls and top with more freshly grated Parmesan.

Olives

Attributes:

HEALING, FERTILITY, POTENCY, FIDELITY, PROTECTION, PROSPERITY, SUCCESS

Associations:

MERCURY, MOON, SUN, MASCULINE

Olive branches symbolize peace and can be hung over the door to protect the household from evil. The olive leaves bring good fortune, prosperity, and security in love and business when carried.

Four Cheese Garlic Cream Pasta

Yield: 4 Servings
Reheats well

- 1 TBSP olive oil
- 1 TBSP butter
- 5 garlic cloves, minced
- 8 oz pkg spaghetti or linguini
- 1 chicken bouillon cube
- 1 cup heavy cream
- ½ cup shredded Mozzarella
- ½ cup shredded white Cheddar
- ½ cup Provolone, chopped small
- ½ cup shredded Parmesan
- ¼ cup sliced green onions

Heat olive oil and butter in a large skillet over medium-low heat. Add minced garlic and cook for about a minute without burning.

Cook pasta in a separate pot, reserving ½ cup of cooked pasta water before draining and dissolving the chicken bouillon cube in it.

Add to the skillet the pasta water with dissolved bouillon cube, heavy cream, and cooked pasta. Bring to a boil, stirring frequently. Stir in cheeses and continue stirring until cheeses melt and coat pasta – about 1 minute. Reduce heat to low and simmer for about another minute, stirring constantly.

Serve on individual plates and top with sliced green onions.

The sauce is not meant to be thick, but will thicken as it cools on your plate and sticks to the pasta more. The best flavor comes through as it cools a bit.

Celery

Associations:

Masculine,
Mercury, Fire

Magical Uses:

Chew the seeds to aid in concentration or use in spell pillows to induce sleep. Celery seeds increase psychic powers. The stalk, along with the seeds, induces lust when eaten.

Witches supposedly ate celery seeds before flying off on their brooms so they wouldn't become dizzy and fall off.

Grandma's Macaroni & Cheese

Yield: 8 Servings
Reheats well

- 2 cups macaroni, cooked
- 1½ cup extra-sharp Cheddar cheese, shredded
- About 20 slices of extra-sharp Cheddar cheese, slices should be thin, but not paper-thin
- 1 egg beaten
- ¼ cup skim milk
- ½ tsp garlic powder
- ½ tsp onion powder
- ¼ tsp celery salt
- 3 TBSP butter
- Black pepper to taste

Preheat the oven to 350° F.

Shred and slice the cheese.

Cook macaroni according to package directions.

In a small mixing bowl, beat the egg. Add milk and seasonings and whisk until well blended.

Drain macaroni. Add the butter to the pan you cooked the macaroni in and return the drained macaroni to the pan, stirring in the shredded cheese until well blended and all the cheese is melted.

Pour macaroni into a greased 9 x 9 or larger baking dish. Top with cheese slices to cover the entire top of the casserole, right up to the edges of the dish. Pour egg mixture over the top, then sprinkle black pepper over the top.

Bake for 30 minutes or until the top starts to brown lightly.

Tomatoes

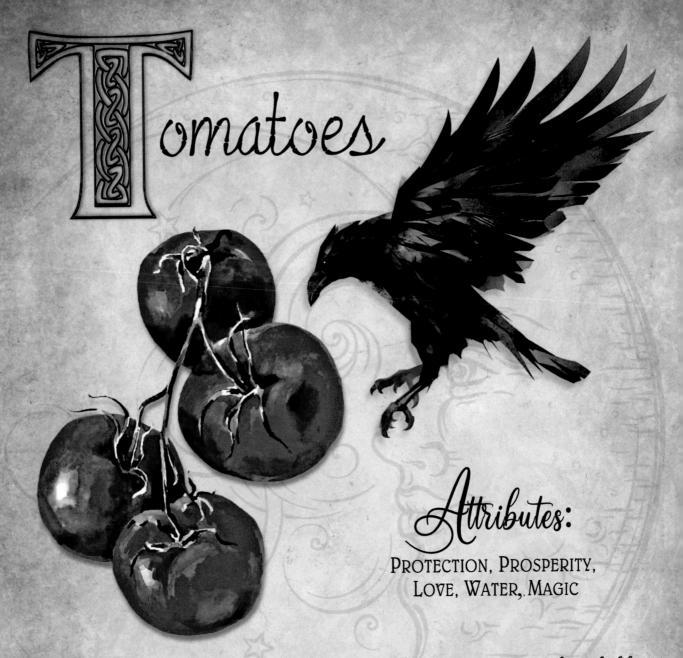

Attributes:
PROTECTION, PROSPERITY,
LOVE, WATER, MAGIC

Placing a large red tomato on the mantel will bring prosperity to a household. (Be sure to change it every three days.) If a tomato is placed on a windowsill it repels evil from entering. Tomato plants in the garden, with their bright yellow flowers and red fruit, have a protective effect. Eat tomatoes, or include them in a romantic supper, to inspire love.

Homemade Spaghetti Sauce

Yield: 8 Servings
Reheats and freezes well

- 1 lb ground beef
- 1 cup chopped onion
- 1 green pepper, chopped
- 3 cloves garlic, minced
- 2 24 oz jars Simply Ragu® Traditional Pasta Sauce (Bertolli® Tomato & Basil is a nice alternative)
- 1 tsp oregano
- 1 tsp Penzey's® Tuscan Sunset Seasoning
- Lots of fresh grated Parmesan cheese

Brown ground beef in a large soup pot or Dutch oven.

Stir in onion, green pepper, and garlic and sauté until vegetables are translucent and aromatic.

Stir in pasta sauce and seasonings. Simmer for 30 minutes, stirring occasionally.

Cook pasta according to package directions . Serve over hot cooked spaghetti or linguini noodles and top with fresh grated Parmesan cheese.

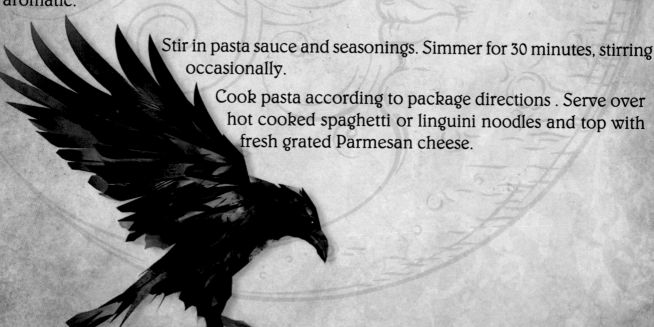

Your Magic Skills

Fire

ARIES
LEO
SAGITTARIUS

Water

CANCER
SCORPIO
PISCES

Air

GEMINI
LIBRA
AQUARIUS

Earth

TAURUS
VIRGO
CAPRICORN

CANDLE MAGIC
PURIFICATION
MANIPULATION OF
ENERGY
HEALING

MIRROR MAGIC
ILLUSIONS
MANIPULATION OF
DREAMS
DIVINATION

KNOT MAGIC
CONTACTING SPIRITS
REMOTE VIEWING
ASTRAL PROJECTION

CRYSTAL MAGIC
RUNES
PROTECTION
MANIPULATION OF
NATURE
KINDRED ANIMALS

Tomato Butter Pasta

Yield: 2 - 4 Servings
Reheats well

- 9 oz spaghetti, linguini, or fettuccini noodles
- 1 28 oz can crushed tomatoes
- 4 TBSP butter
- ½ cup fresh grated Parmesan
- 2 cloves garlic, minced
- 1 handful fresh basil leaves, finely diced
- ¼ tsp chili flakes
- Salt and pepper to taste

Melt 3½ TBSP butter in a large pan over medium heat (save the remaining ½ TBSP butter for later). Add in garlic and chili flakes and sauté for 2 - 3 minutes. Pour in tomatoes, generously season with salt and pepper and give it a good stir.

Keep on a gentle simmer and occasionally stir for 15 minutes or until the sauce begins to thicken and emulsify with the butter.

Meanwhile, cook the pasta in heavily salted water and cook until al dente.

Use tongs to transfer the pasta straight into the pan and toss it to combine with the sauce. Add basil, then toss in parmesan, adding starchy pasta water from the pot (1 TBSP at a time) to thin out the sauce as needed. If you go overboard with the pasta water, just continue to simmer and toss the pasta in the sauce until it thickens and clings around the pasta.

Add in the final ½ TBSP of butter and toss until melted. Serve with additional Parmesan and/or basil if desired.

Basil

Attributes:

Prosperity,
Abundance,
Communication,
Luck

Associations:

Masculinity,
Scorpio, Fire

Sprinkle a few basil leaves in your bath to help you relax.

Basil invites understanding between people.

Keep a basil leaf in your wallet to attract money.

Linguini with Pesto Sauce
~ You Will Need a Food Processor for this Recipe ~

Yield: 4 Servings
Leftover refrigerated sauce can be served over hot fresh linguini

- 3 packed cups fresh basil, stems removed
- 4 large cloves of garlic, peeled
- ½ tsp salt
- 1 cup fresh grated Parmesan cheese
- ¼ cup Pine nuts
- ½ cup olive oil
- ½ tsp parsley flakes
- ½ tsp ground black pepper
- Fresh grated Parmesan for topping
- 8 oz linguini noodles

Puree all ingredients, except linguini, in a food processor until it becomes a uniform paste.

Cook linguini according to package directions.

Toss room temperature pesto with hot, drained pasta noodles–about 3 TBSP per serving, and sprinkle plated servings lightly with fresh grated Parmesan.

Gemelli Pasta

If you dream of eating pasta with friends, it means you feel you are in a comfortable environment, surrounded by good company. This dream is an indication that you will receive good news, visits from friends and family, good times with loved ones, or even dreams coming true.

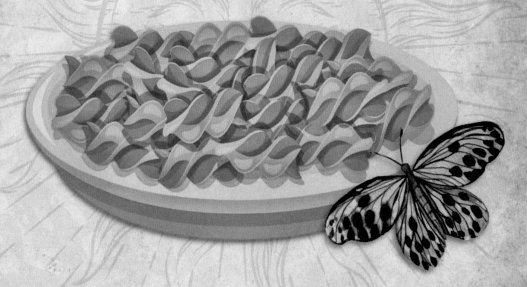

If you dream of eating pasta alone, it is related to your professional life. It indicates that you are looking for prosperity in that chosen field. You feel a need to improve your professional skills. Show your strength and adopt postures that will benefit you in this field.

Gemelli with Crispy Bread Crumbs

Yield: 4 Servings
Does not reheat well

- 12 oz uncooked Gemelli pasta
- 1 TBSP extra virgin olive oil
- ½ cup Italian seasoned Panko® bread crumbs
- ½ cup grated Parmesan cheese
- 1 jar (15 oz) Bertolli® Alfredo with Aged Parmesan Cheese Sauce

Cook pasta in salted water according to package directions.

Meanwhile, heat oil in a small nonstick skillet on medium-low heat. Add bread crumbs and cook 3 - 5 min. or until golden brown, stirring frequently. Remove the skillet from heat, stir in cheese and let cool in the skillet.

Drain pasta and return to pot; stir in Alfredo.

Stir half the crumb mixture into the warm pasta. Sprinkle the remaining crumb mixture over each serving

.

Sour Cream

Dreaming about sour cream means you will overcome the difficulties you are experiencing. You are pushing your feelings back inside rather than expressing them. You need to make the first move in a relationship.

You are flipping back and forth on a decision and unwillingly going along with a plan. This dream is a message to find more information about a particular situation.

Associations:
KINDNESS, COMPASSION, GENTLENESS

Quiche Lorraine

Yield: 6 Servings
Reheats well

- 1 refrigerated pie crust
- 1½ cups grated extra-sharp Cheddar cheese
- 4 eggs
- ½ cup milk
- ½ cup sour cream
- ½ cup diced onion
- 1 cup diced, cooked ham

Preheat the oven to 375° F.

Butter the quiche dish and place the pie crust in it.

Place grated cheese on the bottom. It should be a thick layer. Sprinkle on the ham, then the onions.

In a large mixing bowl, whisk the eggs, milk, and sour cream until well blended and pour over the top of the quiche.

Bake for 45 minutes to one hour. It should be firm before removing it from the oven. Let cool 5 minutes before cutting and serving.

Note: Use this basic quiche custard for your own creations by replacing the ham with sausage or several of your favorite sautéed veggies and cheeses, using the measurements above as a guideline. Squashes, tomatoes, and mushrooms are excellent quiche veggies. If you're altering the cheese choice, use hard cheeses, not soft ones like Mozzarella and Havarti. If you want to add herbs and spices to your creations, add them to the custard.

Black Pepper

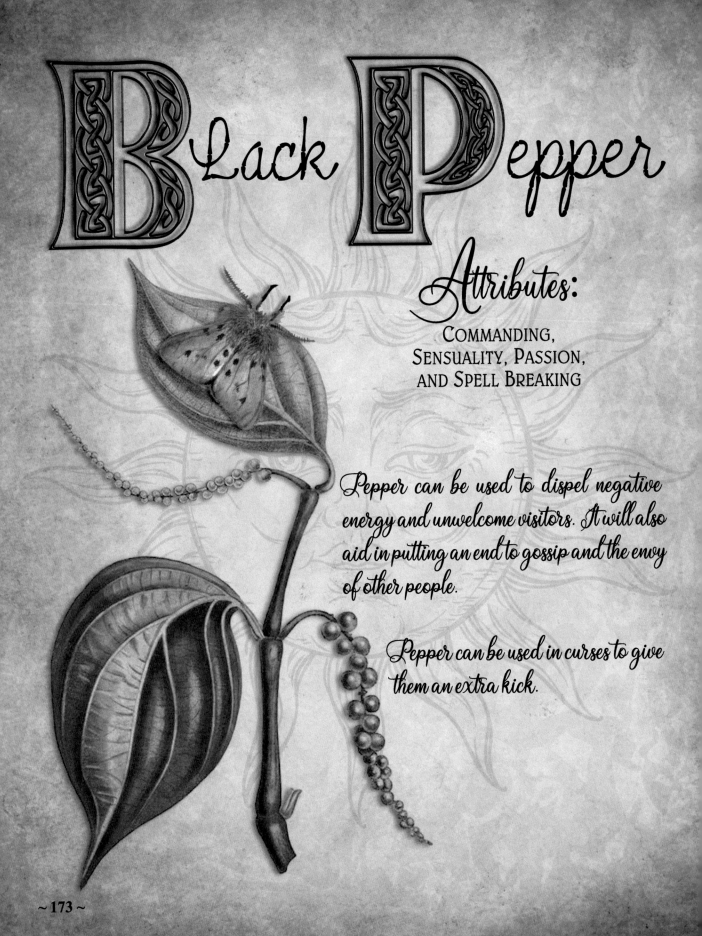

Attributes:

COMMANDING,
SENSUALITY, PASSION,
AND SPELL BREAKING

Pepper can be used to dispel negative energy and unwelcome visitors. It will also aid in putting an end to gossip and the envy of other people.

Pepper can be used in curses to give them an extra kick.

Polish Cabbage, Noodles & Sausage

Yield: 4 - 6 Servings
Reheats well

- 1 pkg Eckrich® Turkey Smoked Skinless Sausage, sliced into ¼-inch discs
- 2 TBSP olive oil
- ¼ cup salted butter
- 1 cup onion, diced
- 1 clove of garlic, minced
- ½ - ¾ head of green cabbage, coarsely chopped
- 1 cup Gemelli pasta (or other small pasta)
- ⅛ tsp red pepper flakes
- ¼ tsp black pepper
- Salt to taste
- Water, as needed

Cook pasta noodles according to package directions, drain and set aside.

In a large, deep skillet, heat olive oil over medium heat and sauté sausage until brown. Add butter, onion, and garlic and cook until onions become translucent. Stir in cabbage, peppers, salt, and water so that it's about an inch deep in the bottom of the skillet. Cover and reduce heat to low; simmer until cabbage is soft and wilted (about 20 - 25 minutes). Stir frequently, adding water as needed to avoid sticking and burning, especially if using a skillet without a non-stick surface.

Stir in pasta and cook another minute or two to reheat the pasta. Serve.

pinach

Spinach represents strength and endurance. Because of its lightness, it helps you connect with your inner child

Associations:

JUPITER,
EARTH, FEMININE

Attributes:

PASSION, FERTILITY,
STRENGTH, ABUNDANCE,
PROSPERITY

Chicken Taquitos

Yield: 15 - 20 Taquitos
Does not reheat well

- 2 cups cooked shredded chicken (I use rotisserie)
- 6 oz cream cheese, softened
- ¼ cup store-bought salsa
- ¼ cup sour cream
- 1 cup shredded cheddar cheese
- 1 cup baby spinach leaves, chopped
- ¼ tsp cumin
- ¼ tsp garlic powder
- ¼ tsp chili powder
- Salt and freshly ground black pepper to taste
- 15 - 20 soft flour tortillas

  For Serving
- Guacamole, sour cream, salsa, hot sauce

In a medium size mixing bowl, add cream cheese, salsa, and sour cream and stir until smooth. Add remaining ingredients (except tortillas) and toss to combine.

Place a large spoonful of filling in a line along the center of each tortilla and roll tightly. Secure with a toothpick if needed.

Baked Taquitos: Preheat oven to 425° F. Lightly brush tortillas with olive oil and bake for 15 - 20 minutes or until the shells are crispy.

Fried Taquitos: Add about 1½ inch of oil to a large skillet and heat to medium-high. Once hot (the tortillas should sizzle immediately when added to the oil), fry the taquitos in small batches for a few seconds on each side, rotating them as they cook, until they are golden and crispy on all sides. Place them on a paper towel-lined plate.

Serve with guacamole, salsa, and sour cream for dipping or topping.

Enchiladas

Dreaming about enchiladas means if you can visualize success, then you will achieve success. You also need to incorporate more joy, amusement, and relaxation into your life.

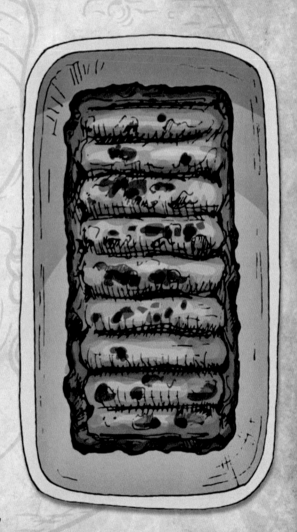

You will take command at work and home; you are doing precisely what you need to do at this moment. Life is unpredictable. Work out simple solutions to unpredictable problems, and everything will work out.

Beef Enchiladas

Yield: 4 Servings
Reheats well

- 2 tsp olive oil
- 1½ lbs. ground beef
- ½ cup onion finely diced
- 1 tsp minced garlic
- 1 packet of taco seasoning
- 1 TBSP water
- 2 10-ounce cans of red enchilada sauce
- 2½ cups shredded cheddar cheese, divided use
- 10 flour tortillas 8-inch size
- ½ cup sliced black olives
- ¼ cup sliced green onions
- cooking spray
- sour cream for topping (optional)

Preheat the oven to 350° F. Coat a 9 x 13 pan with cooking spray.

Heat oil in a large skillet over medium-high heat. Add the ground beef and cook for 3 - 4 minutes or until cooked through. Add the onion and cook for 4 - 5 minutes or until the onion has softened. Add the garlic and cook for 30 seconds. Add the taco seasoning, along with 1 TBSP of water. Stir until everything is coated in seasoning.

Spread 1 cup of enchilada sauce over the bottom of the baking pan.

On a separate work surface, place 1½ TBSP of cheese down the center of each tortilla, then divide the beef mixture evenly among the tortillas.

Roll up each tortilla tightly and arrange it in the baking dish.

Pour 1 cup of enchilada sauce over the tops of the tortilla rolls. Sprinkle the remaining cheese over the sauce.

Bake for 20 minutes or until cheese has melted and sauce is bubbling.

Top with olives and green onions, and serve. Sour cream is also a nice topping if you want a richer dish.

Paprika

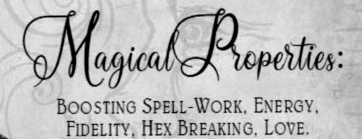

Magical Properties:

Boosting Spell-Work, Energy,
Fidelity, Hex Breaking, Love.

Beef, Black Bean & Corn Quesadillas

Yield: 8 Servings
Reheats well

- 1 8-oz package of large flour tortillas (for burritos)
- 1 lb ground beef
- 1 cup chopped onion
- 1 green pepper, chopped
- 1 can of black beans
- 1 can of corn
- 1 can of diced tomatoes
- 1 pkg Taco Seasoning
- 12 oz pkg shredded Mozzarella cheese
- Olive oil
- Sour cream for dipping or topping

Brown ground beef in a large skillet. Stir in onion and green pepper and sauté for 2 - 3 minutes. Stir in corn, black beans, and tomatoes (do not drain liquid from the cans). Stir in Taco Seasoning. Cover and simmer for 10 - 15 minutes, stirring occasionally.

Heat a second non-stick skillet on low heat. Pour olive oil onto a paper towel and coat the inside of the skillet with the oil using the paper towel. Do not pour oil directly into the skillet, as the tortilla will absorb too much.

Place a tortilla in the skillet and allow it to warm for about a minute. Spoon about ¼ cup of the beef mixture onto one side of the tortilla and top with a generous amount of mozzarella cheese (3 - 4 TBSPs). Using a spatula, flip the empty side of the tortilla over the beef and cheese mixture and lightly hold the spatula on it for a few seconds to melt the cheese a little. Slide the quesadilla onto a plate directly from the pan. Repeat this process for each quesadilla.

Serve with sour cream for dipping or topping. Guacamole also makes an excellent topping.

Carrots

Magical Properties:

Carrots have long been used in love and lust spells. Used to aid fertility. Carrots are also tied to the solar plexus chakra, bringing high energy and creative flow. It can help you put projects into action while keeping you grounded.

Associations:

MARS,
MASCULINE,
FIRE

Attributes:

FERTILITY,
CLARITY

Bim Bim Bap

Yield: 2 - 4 Servings
Reheats well

- 2 cups cooked long grain rice (Mahatma brand is excellent)
- 4 eggs, fried soft (runny yolks)
- 1 can of black beans, drained
- 1 cup Julienne style carrots (bagged this way in the produce section)
- 1 cup bean sprouts
- 1 cup onion, chopped
- ½ cup Mr. Yoshida's® Original Gourmet Sweet Teriyaki Marinade
- 1 TBSP Honey
- 2 TBSP Butter

Prepare rice according to package directions, so you have 2 cups of cooked rice.

Heat black beans in a small saucepan.

Melt 2 TBSP butter in a saucepan and add a TBSP of honey and sauté carrots until crisp and tender.

Sauté bean sprouts lightly in butter in a separate small sauté pan until crisp and tender. It doesn't take much – this is mainly for flavor and heating. Remove from heat, set aside, and keep warm.

Sauté onions in the same pan as the bean sprouts until crisp-tender. Set aside and keep warm.

Fry eggs in butter in a large skillet while heating ½ cup of Teriyaki sauce in the microwave.

Assembly: Split the rice into 2 to 4 serving bowls. Place two fried eggs in the center of each bowl on top of the rice. Add veggies one at a time around the eggs, so it looks like individual servings around the edges of the bowl. Drizzle Teriyaki sauce over each bowl to your desired flavor. Some people like a lot of sauce, and some like just a little.

Peanuts

Attributes:
JUPITER,
MASCULINE

Magical Properties:
Wealth, Prosperity, Stability, Energy,
Grounding, Protection against
loss from abuse or neglect.

Easy-Pad Thai

Yield: 4 Servings
Does not reheat well

- 12 oz rice noodles
- 3 - 4 boneless chicken breasts
- 1 bottle of store-bought Teriyaki Sauce
- 1 cup bean sprouts
- 3 scrambled eggs
- 4 green onions, sliced
- 1 cup chopped peanuts
- ½ tsp cilantro

Pad Thai Sauce

- ⅓ cup soy sauce
- 2 TBSP Sriracha sauce
- ¼ cup lime juice
- ¼ cup canola oil
- ¼ cup brown sugar

Place washed chicken in the slow cooker and cover with teriyaki sauce. Cover and cook on low for 6 hours. Cut into bite-size pieces and keep warm.

Prepare noodles according to package instructions.

Whisk together ingredients for Pad Thai sauce and heat over low heat while noodles are cooking. Scramble eggs in a non-stick skillet without butter or oil, and break them up well.

Drain noodles and place in a large bowl; toss in chicken, sprouts, eggs, cilantro, and Pad Thai sauce. Top with green onions and chopped peanuts.

Rice

Attributes:

MONEY, PROSPERITY, FERTILITY, PROTECTION, SECURITY

Healing:

In ancient times rice was used to heal swelling, exhaustion, hangovers, and much more! Eat them when you are feeling ill.

The tradition of throwing rice at newly married couples is meant to impart blessings of fertility, abundance, and prosperity.

Korean BBQ Chicken

Yield: 4 - 6 Servings
Reheats well

- 2 - 3 boneless, skinless chicken breasts
- 1 bottle Chung Jung One® Korean BBQ Sauce or another brand of your choice
- 1 bunch of green onions, sliced
- Mahatma extra long grain rice

Wash chicken breasts and place them in a slow cooker. Pour the entire bottle of Korean BBQ sauce over the chicken. Cover and cook on low for 6 hours.

Cook rice according to package directions about 20 minutes before you're ready to remove the chicken from the slow cooker.

Slice the green onions.

Remove chicken and shred with 2 forks on a large cutting board. Strain the sauce in the slow cooker over a medium size bowl to remove any debris from the sauce.

Serve the chicken over the rice. Drizzle generously with the sauce and sprinkle green onions over the top.

Side Dishes

Cauliflower

Use cauliflower during your Full Moon rituals. The cauliflower is associated with protection.

Due to the connection to the feminine and the moon, it can be utilized in spells dealing with calming and regulating emotions. Eat to emphasize feminine energies and help you initiate lunar rites and cycles.

Associations:

FEMALE, WATER,
MOON, HEART CHAKRA

Roasted Garlic Parmesan Cauliflower

Yield: 4 - 6 Servings
Reheats well

- 1 medium size head cauliflower
- 2 garlic cloves, minced
- ¼ tsp black pepper
- ¼ tsp salt
- 1 cup Italian seasoned breadcrumbs
- ½ cup butter, melted
- ½ cup fresh grated Parmesan cheese

Preheat the oven to 400° F. Line a baking sheet with parchment paper and set aside.

Cut the cauliflower into florets, all roughly the same size.

Melt butter in a medium bowl and stir in garlic.

Combine breadcrumbs, salt, pepper, and Parmesan cheese in another medium bowl and stir until well blended.

Stir cauliflower florets into the garlic butter mixture until well coated, then roll each floret in the breadcrumb mixture and place on the baking sheet.

Roast in 400° F oven for 30 - 35 minutes or until golden brown.

Cream Cheese

To dream of cream cheese means you are accepting yourself the way you are.

These dreams indicate you feel your life is running smoothly and you feel successful in the pursuit of your goals.

Irish Potato Casserole

Yield: 8 Servings
Reheats well

- 10 medium to large potatoes, peeled and cut into cubes
- 8 oz cream cheese, softened
- 8 oz sour cream
- ½ cup butter, melted
- ¼ cup fresh chives, chopped
- 1 clove of garlic, minced
- 1 tsp salt
- 1 tsp pepper
- ⅛ tsp garlic powder
- Paprika

Cook potatoes in boiling, salted water for approximately 20 minutes or until tender. Drain.

Preheat the oven to 350° F.

In a large mixing bowl, add drained potatoes and all remaining ingredients except the paprika. Beat with an electric mixer until smooth.

Spoon mixture into a lightly buttered 2-quart casserole and sprinkle lightly with paprika.

Bake at 350° F for 30 minutes.

Counting Crows

One for sorrow.

Two for joy.

Three for a girl.

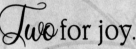

Four for a boy.

Five for silver.

Six for gold.

Seven for a secret never told.

Eight for a wish.

Nine for a kiss.

Ten for a time of joyous bliss.

Cheddar Sweet Corn Pie

Yield: 6 - 8 Servings
Reheats well

- 2 TBSP butter (plus extra for the dish)
- 1 cup finely chopped yellow onion
- 1 medium garlic clove, minced
- 4 cups fresh or thawed corn kernels (6 large ears)
- ⅔ cup milk
- 2 cups grated Cheddar cheese, divided
- ¾ cup Panko® bread crumbs
- 1 tsp Kosher salt
- ¾ tsp ground white pepper
- 3 TBSP chopped fresh chives, optional
- 3 eggs
- Paprika (optional)

Preheat oven to 375° F and move the rack above the middle position. Lightly butter a standard-sized pie plate.

Melt 1½ TBSP butter in a medium skillet over medium-high heat. Add onion and cook for about 4 minutes, until slightly browned at the edges. Turn heat down to medium, add garlic, and cook 2 - 3 minutes, until garlic is fragrant but not browned. Combine onion/garlic mixture in a medium mixing bowl with corn, milk, 1½ cups cheese, ½ cup Panko, salt and pepper, and chives. After stirring, add eggs and mix well. Pour mixture into prepared pan.

Melt remaining ½ TBSP butter, let cool slightly, then combine with ¼ cup Panko®, ½ cup cheese, ½ TBSP chives, and a pinch of salt and pepper. Sprinkle over the pie filling. Bake for about 35 minutes, until slightly puffed, set, and beginning to brown. Cool for 5 - 10 minutes before serving, and top with a dash of paprika and more chives, if desired.

The pie keeps well when prepared and baked in advance.

Cornmeal

A mixture of salt, cornmeal, and ceremonial ash can be placed outside your home for protection.

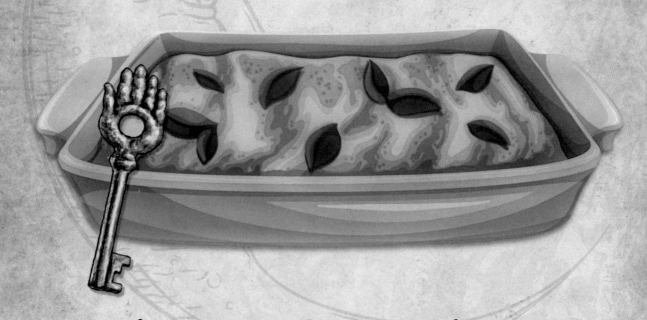

Attributes:

WEALTH,
ABUNDANCE,
PROTECTION

Associations:

FIRE, SUN,
FEMININE

POLENTA WITH SMOKED PAPRIKA & CHEDDAR

Yield: 8 - 10 Servings
Reheats well

- 1 box Delallo® Instant Polenta (9.2 oz)
- 2 32 oz boxes Kitchen Basics® Chicken Stock
- ½ tsp smoked paprika
- ¾ cup extra-sharp Cheddar cheese

Cook polenta according to package directions, substituting the water with chicken stock. When all liquid is absorbed, stir in smoked paprika and Cheddar cheese.

This dish makes a lot of polenta. The best way to save and reheat polenta is to pour leftovers into tall drinking glasses, cover with saran wrap and refrigerate. Run a butter knife along the inside of the glass to loosen it and keep the "loaf" intact. Slice the loaf into round patties and sauté in olive oil or butter. Top with a small amount of shredded cheese.

If your main dish or entrée is beef, you can use beef stock instead of chicken stock.

If polenta is the main dish, you can cook it with half water and half milk for a much richer dish, and you can top it with sautéed veggies and shredded cheese.

$\mathcal{P}$anko (Bread Crumbs)

Travel Protection Spell: You will need bread crumbs, a small pouch or Ziplock® bag, house or car key, and a bowl.

The night before your trip, pour the bread crumbs into your bowl and place your house or car keys in the bowl. The next morning, remove your key(s) and place the breadcrumbs in a bag/pouch. Place the pouch in your car or purse and dump the remaining crumbs near your front door or garage. As you do this, speak the following:

Near or far and wherever I roam. My travels will bring me safely back home.

Baked Parmesan Zucchini

Yield: 6 Servings
Reheats well

- ½ tsp dried basil
- ½ tsp garlic powder
- ½ tsp dried oregano
- ½ tsp dried thyme
- ½ cup fresh grated Parmesan cheese
- ½ cup Panko® Breadcrumbs
- 2 Zucchini, cut into strips
- Salt and pepper to taste

Preheat the oven to 350˚ F. Line a baking sheet with parchment paper and set aside.

Cut zucchini in half, width-wise, then slice each half lengthwise into approximately 6 strips. Place on a baking sheet so that all strips are touching each other. Sprinkle with salt and pepper.

In a small bowl, combine spices, Panko®, and Parmesan. Stir until well blended. Sprinkle heavily over zucchini.

Place in the oven on the middle rack and bake for 15 minutes. Then broil for 1 - 2 minutes. Serve immediately.

Witches House Rule #1

Do NOT Bring Spirits Into The House
Unless They Come In a Bottle.

Garlic Mushroom-Cauliflower Skillet

Yield: 4 - 6 Servings
Does not reheat well

- 4 TBSP unsalted butter
- 1 TBSP olive oil
- ½ onion, chopped
- ½ head cauliflower, cut into florets
- 1 pound of mushrooms, cleaned
- 2 TBSP low sodium vegetable stock
- 1 tsp of fresh dried thyme
- 2 TBSP parsley
- 4 cloves garlic, minced
- Salt and pepper to taste

Heat the butter and oil in a large skillet over medium-high heat. Sauté the onion until softened (about 3 minutes).

Add the mushrooms and cook for about 4-5 minutes on all sides. Make sure the mushrooms render as much moisture as possible. Brown them a little more, if necessary, to avoid them becoming soggy at the end. Keep an eye on it, so they don't burn.

Once mushrooms are well browned, add cauliflower florets. Cook until golden and crispy on the edges, about 8 - 10 minutes. Veggies must be well-browned.

Pour in the vegetable stock and cook for 2 minutes, reducing the sauce slightly.

Add thyme, 1 TBSP of parsley, and garlic. Cook for a minute until fragrant. Season with salt and pepper to taste, sprinkle with remaining parsley, and serve.

Mabon

The holiday of "Mabon" is a harvest festival and coincides with the Autumn Equinox, the time when night and day stand equal; it is a time to honor a moment of balance and express gratitude for the fruits of the earth.

It's a time of gratitude when we reflect on the successes of the previous year and recognize the need to share our harvest during the coming winter months.

We celebrate the gifts of the earth and give thanks for the summer's abundance and pay tribute to the winter ahead.

Pay tribute to Mabon by creating a display of Fall things: apples, pine cones, acorns, leaves, pomegranate, squash, and root vegetables. Focus on the Mabon colors: red, orange, maroon, brown, and gold. Light a candle and meditate on the abundance you have in your life

Oven Roasted Carrots

Yield: 4 Servings
Reheats well

- 5 medium to large carrots, peeled and sliced on the diagonal, about 1 inch thick
- 2 TBSP olive oil
- Salt and pepper

Move the oven rack up as far up as it can go in the oven. Preheat the oven to 450° F.

Line a baking sheet with foil.

Place carrots in a Ziploc® bag with olive oil and shake to coat. Pour them out onto the baking sheet and spread them out for even cooking. Sprinkle with salt and pepper.

Place in the oven on the top rack for 15 minutes. Serve immediately.

Pineapple

Attributes:

Hospitality, Prosperity, Luck, Courage, Confidence, and Chastity

Associations:

Fire, Sun, Masculine

Dried pineapple makes for excellent sachets and incenses that can draw wealth to the home and encourage financial gain. Likewise, once you've finished cutting your pineapple, you can turn the pineapple crown into a plant that attracts good fortune.

Pineapple Basmati Rice

Yield: 2 Servings
Does not reheat well

- 1 TBSP butter
- ½ can pineapple chunks, drained
- ¾ cup of water
- ½ cup Basmati rice
- Salt and pepper to taste

Melt butter in a small pot over medium-high heat. Add pineapple chunks, tossing occasionally for 1 minute. Stir in water, rice, salt and pepper. Bring to a boil, then reduce heat to low, cover, and simmer until all water is absorbed.

Green Beans

When you are snapping green beans in a dream, that symbolizes jealousy and envy. It is possible that someone you know has achieved everything that you wanted in life. Instead of trying to succeed, you torment yourself with the fact they are in a better position than you

If you are eating green beans in a dream, that symbolizes joy. You have balance in your life and enough time to dedicate yourself to both business and personal obligations. You radiate positive energy and attract people similar to your mood. Your friends will enjoy your company and look forward to seeing you.

Easy Weeknight Green Beans

Yield: 2 Servings
Does not reheat well

- ½ pound fresh green beans, trimmed & washed
- 2 TBSP water
- 1 TBSP butter
- 1 tsp Penzey's® Sandwich Sprinkle

Place trimmed green beans in medium microwave-safe bowl with 2 TBSP water. Cover with plastic wrap and poke a few holes in the plastic wrap for venting. Microwave on high until crisp-tender, about 5 - 6 minutes. Drain and toss with butter and Penzey's® Sandwich Sprinkle.

A Wiccan Blessing

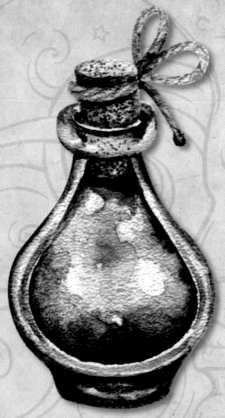

Smoke of Air, and Fire of Earth,

Cleanse and bless

this home and hearth.

Drive away

all harm and fear,

Only good

may enter here.

Easy Vegetable Medley

Yield: 4 Servings
Reheats well

- 1 cup chopped fresh cauliflower
- 1 cup chopped fresh broccoli
- 1 cup sliced fresh carrots
- 3 TBSP butter
- 1 TBSP honey
- Water
- A few dashes of pepper

Melt butter in a large skillet over medium heat. Drizzle in honey. Toss in vegetables and a few dashes of pepper. Add enough water to cover the bottom of the pan. Stir and sauté until crisp-tender (about 10 minutes), adding water as needed if it's evaporating too quickly.

Yellow Squash

Dreaming about yellow squash represents your need for more self-discipline in your life. You are looking for guidance in your subconscious. This dream indicates your changing emotional feelings.

Expect changes in your relationship, especially in terms of the boundaries you may have placed on yourselves. Move beyond your self-imposed limitations and begin to explore new dimensions and new options for your future together.

Yellow Squash

Yield: 4 Servings
Reheats well

- 4 medium yellow squash
- ½ medium onion, sliced, separate rings
- 3 TBSP butter
- 1 TBSP honey
- ¼ tsp black pepper
- Dash of salt
- Water

Melt butter in a large, deep skillet over medium-high heat, and drizzle in the honey. Toss in the squash and onions, salt, and pepper. Add enough water to cover the bottom of the skillet, about an inch deep. Cover and reduce heat to medium or medium-low. Allow to simmer for approximately 20 minutes, stirring occasionally. Don't let the skillet go dry. Add small amounts of water as needed until done. Squash should be soft and wilted.

Connecting to the Moon

Waning Crescent Moon

Surrender

Recuperate and rest.
It is a time to heal and rejuvenate.

Sweet Jiffy® Mix Cornbread

Yield: 9 Squares

- 1 box Jiffy® Corn Muffin Mix
- 1 egg
- ⅓ cup milk
- 1 TBSP vanilla extract
- 2 tsp sugar
- 2 tsp Canola oil

Preheat the oven to 400° F. Grease a 9 x 9 baking dish with butter.

In a medium mixing bowl, stir all ingredients together until well blended. Pour evenly into greased baking dish and bake at 400° for 15 - 20 minutes. Serve immediately.

To reheat, sprinkle a few drops of water over the cornbread, and cover with plastic wrap. Poke a few holes into the wrap. Microwave for one minute.

Cheddar Cheese

If you are enjoying the cheese in your dream, it is representative of happiness and fulfillment. Your dream may even suggest that you return to the simpler things in life to get the most enjoyment.

If a mouse is eating cheese, this can show that things are not what they seem. A rodent indicates theft or a sneaky or untrue personality, so if a mouse is in possession of the cheese, it represents someone close to you who is sneaky or deceptive.

Scalloped Tomatoes

Yield: 6 Servings
Reheats well

- 2 cups chopped onion
- 2 TBSP butter
- 1 20 oz can diced tomatoes
- 3 slices whole wheat or multi-grain bread, cubed
- ¼ tsp pepper
- ½ tsp salt (optional)
- 2 TBSP brown sugar
- 1 cup shredded extra-sharp cheddar cheese, divided

Preheat oven to 350° F.

Sauté onions in butter until transparent. Remove from heat and set aside.

In a large mixing bowl, combine tomatoes, bread cubes, ½ cup cheddar, sautéed onions, brown sugar, salt, and pepper.

Pour into a buttered casserole, top with remaining cheddar cheese, and bake at 350° F for 1 hour.

Connecting to the Moon

Emotions and intuition tend to be at a high during this period.
This is a time of increased creativity.

Enjoy the full moon energy and deepen your connection to the Universe.

Roasted Cabbage Steak

Yield: 4 Servings
Does not reheat well

- 1 head of green cabbage cut into 1 inch thick slices
- 1½ TBSP olive oil
- 2 - 3 cloves garlic, minced
- Kosher salt
- Black pepper

Preheat oven to 400° F.

Line baking sheet with aluminum foil. Place cabbage steaks on the baking sheet.

In a small bowl, stir together the olive oil and garlic and brush over cabbage steaks with a silicone pastry brush. Sprinkle each with a pinch of Kosher salt and black pepper.

Roast for 30 minutes. Remove the baking sheet from the oven, flip cabbage steaks, repeat the application of garlic, olive oil, salt, and pepper, and roast for another 30 minutes. Edges should be crispy and brown.

Brussel Sprouts

Dreaming of brussel sprouts represents feelings about needing to act mature or responsible. Choosing to do the right thing on your own. Accepting a mature or adult situation.

Brussel sprouts may reflect a positive attitude about having to be responsible on your own or accept a mature situation. Not running from your problems.

Glazed Brussels Sprouts with Crispy Onions

Yield: 6 Servings
Does not reheat well

- 1 lb fresh brussels sprouts
- Water
- ¼ cup olive oil
- 3 TBSP Bertolli® Balsamic Glaze
- 3 TBSP honey
- 1 cup French's® Caramelized Crispy Fried Onions
- Salt and pepper to taste

Preheat oven to 400° F.

Trim and wash sprouts and place in Ziploc® bag with olive oil, salt, and pepper, and toss to coat. Place on a foil-lined baking sheet.

In a small bowl, whisk balsamic glaze and honey together. Set aside.

Roast sprouts for 20 - 30 minutes until almost tender, shaking pan occasionally. Remove sprouts from the oven, drizzle with balsamic mixture and stir to coat. Roast another 10 minutes.

Transfer sprouts to a serving bowl and sprinkle with crispy onions.

VARIATION: For a quicker version of this recipe, steam or boil sprouts (frozen sprouts are good here also); drain water; stir in balsamic glaze and honey; salt and pepper; and serve topped with crispy onions. This version is great if you're cooking for 2; just cut portions of all ingredients in half.

Witches House Rule #2

NO PARKING of Brooms Outside Because the Neighbors Already Think I'm Odd.

Garlic-Parmesan Roasted Brussels Sprouts

Yield: 4 Servings
Reheats well

- 16 oz Brussels sprouts, rinsed
- 3 TBSP olive oil (or melted butter)
- ½ tsp Kosher salt
- ¼ tsp freshly ground black pepper
- 1 tsp Italian seasoning
- 3 garlic cloves, minced
- ½ cup grated Parmesan cheese

Preheat your oven to 400° F.

Wash and trim the bottom of the Brussels sprouts and slice each one in half, top to bottom. Line a large baking sheet with aluminum foil.

Pat the Brussels sprouts dry with paper towels and place them in a large bowl. Add olive oil, Italian seasoning, garlic, Parmesan, salt, and pepper. Toss gently to coat evenly.

Place the Brussels sprouts on the prepared baking sheet, spreading them evenly into one layer. Bake on a center rack for 25 - 30 minutes. Adjust the time according to your oven. The vegetables should be golden brown, not blackened.

Kitchen Witchery

Herbs and spices that attract money into your life.

Basil

Dill

Cinnamon

Ginger

Spearmint

Allspice

Chamomile

Emily's Corn Pudding

Yield: 6 Servings
Reheats well

- 1 can of corn, drained
- 3 eggs
- 1 cup of milk
- 1 cup of sugar
- 2 TBSP vanilla extract
- ½ tsp cinnamon
- 3 pats butter, softened

Preheat oven to 350° F.

In a large mixing bowl, beat 3 eggs with a whisk. Add milk, sugar, and vanilla, and blend well. Stir in corn.

Pour into greased casserole and sprinkle the top with cinnamon; dot the top with 3 small pats of softened butter.

Bake for 1 hour or until the casserole is set.

Cornbread

There is a strong connection to the family when dreaming of cornbread. It may indicate a feeling of unity, and you are feeling more bonded with them. You are instinctively expecting something to happen which will ultimately improve your family life.

Dreaming about eating cornbread is an indication that you need to be more observant. You are letting opportunities pass you by. This dream could signal the end of a cycle and the pause before the beginning of a new endeavor.

Jiffy® Cornbread Casserole

Yield: 6 - 8 Servings
Reheats well

- 1 box Jiffy® Corn Muffin Mix
- ½ cup butter, melted
- 1 can whole kernel corn, drained
- 1 can cream-style corn
- 1 cup sour cream
- 2 eggs
- 8 oz shredded cheddar cheese, divided

Preheat the oven to 375° F and grease a large size casserole dish.

Beat eggs in a large mixing bowl. Pour in melted butter, both cans of corn (whole kernel and cream style), the Jiffy® Muffin Mix, sour cream, and half the shredded cheese (4 oz). Stir until well blended, then pour into greased casserole dish.

Top with remaining cheese and bake for 50 - 60 minutes or until the center is no longer jiggly.

Milk

Milk is a powerful symbol within most cultural traditions. It is the fluid of eternal life, fertility, and abundance.

Milk symbolizes the MOTHER and it is deeply connected with life itself.

Scalloped Potatoes with Cheese

Yield: 10 Servings
Reheats well

- 4 cloves garlic, minced
- 5 lbs red potatoes, peeled & sliced into ⅛ inch slices
- 6 TBSP butter, melted
- 4 cups grated Gruyere cheese
- 3 cups of milk
- Salt and pepper to taste

Preheat oven to 425° F.

Grease a large baking dish and place a layer of sliced potatoes on the bottom of the dish. Sprinkle with salt and pepper, sprinkle with a light layer of grated Gruyere. Continue layering until all potatoes are gone. The last layer should be the cheese.

Melt butter in a medium saucepan, toss in the garlic and cook for about a minute. Stir in milk and bring to a boil. Pour over potatoes.

Bake for 40 minutes or until set and milk is absorbed.

Witches House Rule #3

The Only Goddess that Lives Here is Me, and I am Completely Undomesticated!

Parmesan Zucchini Bites

Yield: 4 Servings
Reheats well

- 3 medium zucchini
- 1 tsp garlic salt, to taste
- 1 TBSP olive oil
- ½ cup Parmesan cheese, grated
- 1½ tsp paprika

Preheat oven to 450°F and line a baking sheet with aluminum foil.

Trim both ends from the zucchini and slice diagonally into ¼-inch thick slices. Arrange the zucchini slices in a single layer on a baking sheet. Sprinkle zucchini with garlic salt and flip each piece so that the garlic salt is on the bottom.

Brush the tops of the zucchini lightly with olive oil and top each slice with Parmesan cheese. Use as little or as much as you would like, then sprinkle lightly with paprika.

Bake 10 - 15 minutes or just until zucchini is soft and Parmesan is melted and bubbly. Remove from oven and allow zucchini to cool about 5 minutes before serving.

Green Onions

Attributes:

Prosperity, Stability, Endurance, Protection, Banishing Negative Influences, Ending Bad Habits, and Removing Illness. healing Money, Prophetic Dreams, and Lust are also associated with Green Onions.

Use this many-layered food to peel away problems in life and dispel anger. The onion is associated with love and is said to increase male virility.

Savory Jasmine Rice

Yield: 2 Servings
Reheats well

- ½ cup Jasmine Rice
- ¾ cup of water
- 1 bunch of green onions, sliced
- 1 TBSP butter
- Salt

In a small saucepan, melt butter. Add green onions and cook until softened, about 1 - 2 minutes. Season with a pinch or two of salt. Pour in water and bring to a boil. Add rice and stir to combine. Cover, reduce heat to low. Simmer until all water is absorbed.

Beets

Beet juice is sometimes used as magical ink and as a substitute for blood in magical use and is known to attract love.

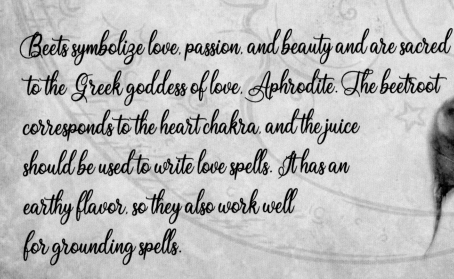

Beets symbolize love, passion, and beauty and are sacred to the Greek goddess of love, Aphrodite. The beetroot corresponds to the heart chakra, and the juice should be used to write love spells. It has an earthy flavor, so they also work well for grounding spells.

Roasted Beets & Sweets in Brown Butter Maple Glaze

Yield: 6 - 8 Servings
Reheats well

- 6 sweet potatoes, peeled and cubed (small, 1-inch-dice)
- 4 beets, peeled and cubed (small, 1-inch-dice)
- 2 TBSP olive oil
- 2 tsp salt
- 1 tsp fresh ground black pepper

For the Glaze
- 1 stick butter
- 2 TBSP real maple syrup
- 3 - 4 fresh thyme sprigs

Preheat the oven to 425° F.

Line 2 baking sheets with aluminum foil and spray with cooking spray.

In a large bowl, toss together the beets, sweet potatoes, salt and pepper. Spread out vegetables on baking sheets and roast in the oven for 30 minutes.

While the potatoes and beets are in the oven, make the brown butter glaze by adding 1 stick of butter to a skillet along with the fresh thyme sprigs. Melt the butter down until just browned (about 5 minutes), then stir in the maple syrup and remove from the heat.

After 30 minutes, remove the potatoes and beets from the oven and toss them with the brown butter glaze. Place back in the oven for 15 minutes, then remove to a large serving bowl and serve hot.

oat Cheese

Dreaming about goat cheese indicates fire, drive, and passion. You need to let go of some unnecessary burdens. You are trying to present the ugly truth in a way that is easier to accept. Your dream is a warning for unexpressed emotions, such as anger. Roll up your sleeves and prepare for some hard work ahead.

You may be experiencing feelings of uncertainty about what the future may hold and preoccupied with discovering something about yourself, your reputation, or your self-identity.

Roasted Carrots with Candied Pecans and Goat Cheese

Yield: 6 - 8 Servings
Reheats well

- 2 lbs. carrots peeled
- ½ cup brown sugar
- 4 TBSP unsalted butter cut into pats
- 1 tsp salt
- ½ tsp pepper
- ½ tsp cinnamon
- 1 cup roughly chopped candied pecans
- 4 oz goat cheese crumbled
- 1 TBSP fresh thyme leaves to garnish

Preheat the oven to 350° F.

Line a baking sheet with foil. Place the carrots in a single layer on the baking sheet. Sprinkle with the brown sugar and evenly distribute the pats of butter. Sprinkle with salt, pepper, and cinnamon.

Place in the oven and bake for 50 - 60 minutes or until the carrots are just fork-tender. During baking, turn the carrots 3 or 4 times.

Once the carrots are cooked, put them in a serving dish. Sprinkle them evenly with the candied pecans and goat cheese. Finish the dish with a sprinkle of fresh thyme leaves.

Kitchen Witchery

Herbs and spices that will bring courage.

Pepper

Basil

Chives

Horseradish

Nettles

Emily's Rice Pudding

Yield: 6 Servings

- 1 cup cooked long grain rice
- 3 eggs
- 1 cup of milk
- 1 cup sugar
- 1½ TBSP vanilla extract
- ½ tsp ground cinnamon
- 3 pats butter, softened

Preheat oven to 350° F.

Cook rice according to package directions.

In a large mixing bowl, beat 3 eggs with a whisk. Add milk, sugar, and vanilla, and blend well. Stir in rice. Pour into greased baking dish and sprinkle the top with cinnamon and dot the top with 3 small pats of softened butter.

Bake for 1 hour or until the casserole is set.

Asparagus

Attributes:

FERTILITY,
PASSION, LUST

Asparagus should be served during Beltane, which is an annual fertility festival. It celebrates fertility, love, and reproduction. Attract a new love or sexual partner. Increase fertility, conception chances, libido, and passion.

Sautéed Asparagus

Yield: 4 Servings
Does not reheat well

- 1 lb fresh asparagus
- 2 TBSP butter
- Salt and pepper to taste
- Water

Wash and trim asparagus.

Melt butter in a large skillet over medium heat. Place asparagus in skillet, sprinkle with salt and pepper. Add a little water to the bottom of the pan, just enough to cover the bottom of the pan. Cook until crisp-tender, about 5 - 6 minutes. You can add more water if it evaporates too quickly.

Peas

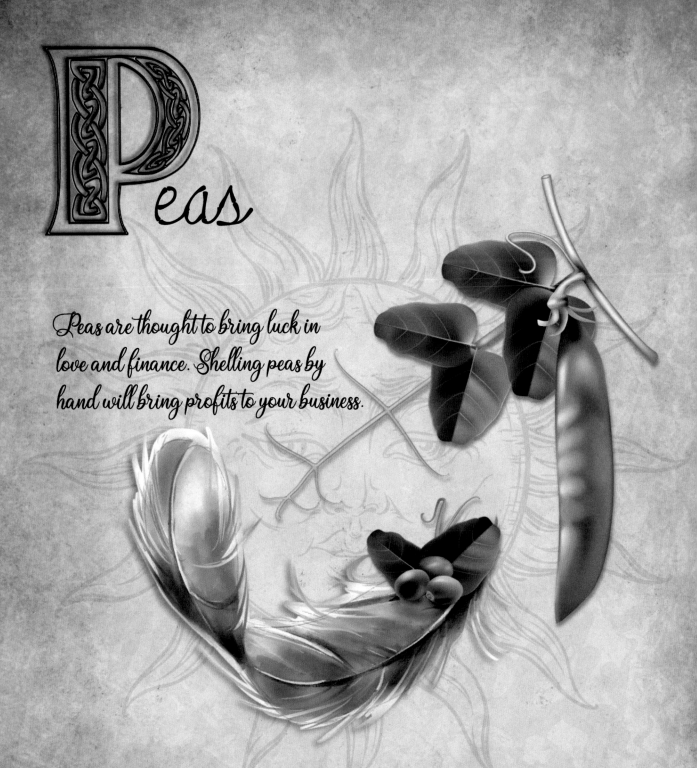

Peas are thought to bring luck in love and finance. Shelling peas by hand will bring profits to your business.

If an unmarried woman finds a pod containing nine peas and hangs it over her door, the next eligible man to walk through it will become her husband.

Risi-Bisi (Peas & Rice)

Yield: 6 Servings
Reheats well

- 1½ cups converted long grain white rice
- ¾ cup chopped onion
- 2 14½ oz cans of low-sodium chicken broth
- ⅓ cup of water
- ¾ tsp Italian seasoning
- ½ tsp basil
- ½ cup frozen baby peas
- ½ cup fresh grated Parmesan cheese

Bring chicken broth and water to a boil in a medium saucepan. Add all ingredients except the cheese and simmer until all liquid is absorbed.

Stir in cheese and serve immediately.

This reheats well, but the cheese loses its flavor overnight, so you may want to add more cheese when reheated.

Holiday Dishes

Tamarind

Carry a tamarind pod or the leaves to attract love.

Attributes:

MULTIPLICITY, RENEWAL, LOVE

Associations:

FEMININE, SATURN, WATER

*Tamarind is a fruit that grows in a pod and is the ingredient in Worchester sauce that gives it that tangy sweet-sour flavor.

Dad's Holiday Glazed Ham

Yield: Approximately 12 Servings
Reheats well or serve cold

- ½ Cure 81 Hormel® Ham
- 3 - 4 TBSP yellow mustard
- 1 ½ cup dark brown sugar
- 1 TBSP ground black pepper
- 2 TBSP Worcestershire® sauce

Preheat oven to 350° F.

In a small bowl, mix all ingredients to create a glaze. Brush over the top and sides of the ham using a pastry brush.

Bake for 1½ hours, basting every 30 minutes.

Nutmeg

Use nutmeg sprinkled in someone's shoe to send unwelcome or problematic people on their way.

*Nutmeg is found in most poultry seasonings.

Associations:

Jupiter,
Archangel Sachiel

Holiday Turkey

Yield: Approximately 12 Servings
Reheats well or serve cold

- 12 - 14 lb Turkey
- 1 Reynolds Oven Cooking Bag®
- 1 TBSP flour
- 1 medium onion, cut into wedges
- 2 TBSP butter, melted
- 1 tsp salt
- ¾ tsp pepper
- 1 tsp poultry seasoning
- 1 tsp garlic powder
- 1 tsp paprika
- ½ tsp ground red pepper
- 1 tsp basil
- ½ tsp ginger

Preheat the oven to 350° F.

Shake flour inside the cooking bag. Place onion wedges in the bottom of the bag.

Wash turkey and pat dry. Brush with melted butter using a silicone pastry brush

Combine seasonings and rub them into the entire turkey.

Slide turkey into the cooking bag and place in a roasting pan. Close the bag with nylon ties that come with the cooking bags and cut a few ½-inch slits in the top of the bag.

Bake according to the size of the turkey (20 minutes per pound) or until legs are loose.

Yule

The best known of the Pagan sabbats, Yule resembles Christmas in many ways, including gift-giving and singing. Yule falls on the Winter Solstice and is a celebration of the shortest day and longest night we will experience in the Northern Hemisphere. However, it's typically celebrated on December 21st. It marks the start of the long winter months and is a time to celebrate the end of the harvest season.

Candles are important in the celebration of this Sabbat, with Yule traditions emphasizing the colors red, green, white, and gold. Images of the Sun are also appropriate. If you have a fireplace, burn a sacred Yule log, but you don't need an actual hearth to brighten your home with candles. Interestingly, many traditions which are generally thought of as belonging to Christmas-including the Yule log, a decorated tree, wreaths, and even caroling-are actually rooted in pre-Christian pagan traditions. So it's quite likely that you've already been celebrating Yule for years, with or without your knowledge!

Easy Holiday Stove Top Stuffing

Yield: 8 Servings
Reheats well

- 32 oz box Kitchen Basics® Chicken Stock
- 1 bag Pepperidge Farm® Herb Seasoned Stuffing Mix
- 2 stalks of celery, chopped
- 1 cup onion, chopped
- ¼ tsp pepper

In a large pan or Dutch oven, mix chicken stock, pepper, celery, and onion. Bring to a boil over high heat. Reduce heat to low, cover, and simmer for 5 minutes.

Stir in stuffing mix, 1 cup at a time, until you reach desired consistency for stuffing. It should be stiff but not dry. You can add more chicken stock (or a little water) if it gets too dry.

Reheat leftovers with a little chicken stock or water to keep it moist.

Pine Nuts

Magical Properties:

Releasing emotions that don't serve you, protection, moving on, resilience, and friendship.

Associations:

Masculine, Air, Mars, Heart chakra, Aquarius

Oven Roasted Garlic Green Beans

Yield: 8 Servings
Reheats well

- 2 lbs fresh green beans, trimmed & washed
- ½ cup pine nuts
- 10 cloves garlic, minced
- 1½ tsp lemon juice
- 1½ tsp Kosher salt
- ½ tsp black pepper
- ¼ tsp sugar
- 6 TBSP olive oil
- ½ cup fresh grated Parmesan cheese

Preheat the oven to 450° F.

In a small skillet, toast pine nuts over medium heat for about 2 minutes. Do not overheat pine nuts as they become quite bitter. Set aside.

Mix beans and remaining ingredients, except the Parmesan, in a large bowl and stir until well blended. Place the beans on a lined baking sheet and roast for 15 minutes, turning once or twice for even cooking.

Place beans in a large serving bowl and toss with pine nuts and Parmesan cheese.

Serve immediately.

Connecting to the Moon

New Moon

New beginnings, a fresh start, a blank page.

"I am open; what I desire I will manifest."

Fancy Sweet Carrots

Yield: 8 Servings
Reheats well

- 6 - 8 large carrots, peeled and sliced
- Water
- 2 TBSP butter
- 2 TBSP honey
- 2 TBSP brown sugar
- 1 tsp cinnamon
- 1 tsp ground ginger

Place carrots in a medium saucepan and add water about an inch or so deeper than the carrots. Add all remaining ingredients and bring to a boil. Reduce heat to low, cover and simmer for 30 - 40 minutes or until carrots are fairly soft.

 Sweet Potatoes

Sweet potatoes are thought to represent warm human relationships.

Carve your name and birth date on a sweet potato and make a wish. Then insert toothpicks into the sweet potato and hang it over a glass of water. Once the potato starts to sprout eyes, you should bake and eat it to make your dreams come true.

Sweet Potato Casserole

Yield: 8 - 10 Servings
Reheats well

- 4 cups cooked Sweet Potatoes (about 8 potatoes)
- 2 eggs, lightly beaten
- ½ cup brown sugar
- ⅓ cup skim milk
- 2 TBSP butter, melted
- 2 TBSP Vanilla

Topping

- ½ cup brown sugar
- ¼ cup flour
- 2 TBSP butter, softened
- ½ cup chopped pecans

Preheat the oven to 350° F.

Wash sweet potatoes and poke some holes in them with a fork. Cook in microwave, 2 potatoes at a time, until done, approximately 10 - 14 minutes.

Allow potatoes to cool, cut in half, and scoop the potato out with a spoon and place into a large mixing bowl. Discard the skins.

Stir in eggs, ½ cup brown sugar, skim milk, 2 TBSP melted butter, and vanilla. Pour mixture into a large greased baking dish.

In a small mixing bowl, combine ½ cup brown sugar, ¼ cup flour, 2 TBSP softened butter, and ½ cup chopped pecans. Stir until crumbly and sprinkle evenly over the top of the potato mixture.

Bake for 30 minutes.

Charging Water

1. Pour water into a bowl.
2. Sprinkle sea salt into the water.
3. Place a clear quartz crystal in the water.
4. Place the bowl on a windowsill to soak up the moonlight (waxing or full).
5. In the morning, pour the water into a bottle and cork it. Use it for blessings, cleansings, or other water spells.

Caramelized Onion and Pecan Brussels Sprouts

Yield: 8 Servings
Reheats well

- 1 medium onion, chopped
- 1 lb Brussels sprouts, trimmed and cut in half
- ¼ cup butter, divided
- 1 cup pecan pieces
- ½ tsp sugar
- 1 tsp salt
- ½ tsp pepper
- ½ - 1 cup water

Melt 2 TBPS butter in a large, heavy skillet over medium-high heat. Add pecans and sauté 5 minutes or until toasted. Remove pecans from the skillet and set aside.

In the same skillet, add more 2 TBSP butter and stir in onions and sugar, stirring often, for 15 minutes or until caramel colored. More butter can be added if needed to prevent sticking. Add back pecans and the Brussels Sprouts, ½ cup water, and cook about 20 minutes, stirring often, until sprouts are crisp-tender. More water can be added if it's boiling off too quickly.

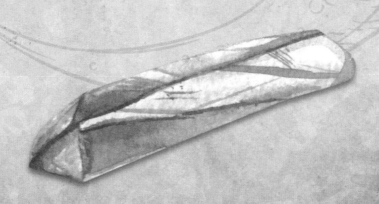

Walnuts

To bring money and prosperity into your life, keep a bowl of walnuts on a table in your home.

Walnuts radiate the power of Jupiter throughout your home bringing new opportunities, fertility and wealth.

Holiday Green Beans with Walnuts

Yield: 10 Servings
Reheats well

This recipe is for a large crowd. Adjust seasonings up or down according to the quantity of beans.

- 4 lbs fresh green beans
- 2 32 oz boxes Kitchen Basic's® Beef Stock
- 2 TBSP minced onion
- 1 tsp salt
- 1½ tsp black pepper
- ¾ cup walnut halves

Wash and trim beans and place in a large saucepan or Dutch oven.

Pour in enough beef stock to cover beans by 2 inches. Add minced onion, salt, and pepper. Bring to a boil, then reduce heat to low, cover, and simmer for 45 minutes. Stir in walnuts and cook an additional 15 minutes. Feel free to add more stock if beans are absorbing too much liquid.

esserts

Cinnamon

Hang a bundle of cinnamon sticks over your front door to guard your home from negative energy and the bad intentions of outsiders.

Add cinnamon to a spell bag or sachet for luck, money drawing, or career success.

Cinnamon is notorious for "heating up" cold romances and igniting passion. If you want to draw passion into your relationship or welcome a new flame into your romantic life, cinnamon attracts sensual energies.

Baked Peaches & Cream

Yield: 8 Servings

- 4 fresh peaches
- Butter
- Honey
- 1 cup mascarpone (mild Italian cream cheese)
- ½ cup heavy whipping cream
- 1 tsp vanilla extract
- Sliced almonds
- Cinnamon sugar

Preheat oven to 350° F.

Cut peaches in half and remove pits, place in a baking dish or cast iron skillet. Place a pat of butter on top of each peach half and drizzle with honey. Bake for 25 - 30 minutes. Keep an eye on them, so they brown but don't burn – cooking time depends on the size of the peaches.

Mix whipping cream, mascarpone, and vanilla extract. Lightly toast almonds in a small skillet over medium heat – do not use oil or butter – this takes about 1 - 2 minutes, and they should be lightly browned.

When peaches are done, place each one on a dessert plate. Spoon any remaining liquid from the baking dish over the peaches. Place a heaping spoonful of mascarpone cream on each peach and top each one with almonds and a sprinkle of cinnamon sugar.

Bananas

Associations:

Masculine, Air, Mars, Leo, Sacral, and Solar Plexus Chakras

Attributes:

Resilience through change, wealth, luck, spirituality, and increased sexual stamina in men

Bananas Foster

- ½ cup unsweetened apple juice
- ⅛ tsp apple pie spice
- 3 ripe bananas, peeled and cut into thirds, then split each piece lengthwise
- 1¼ tsp cornstarch
- 1 tsp Rum
- ⅛ tsp maple flavoring
- ⅛ tsp butter flavoring
- Vanilla ice cream or frozen yogurt

Combine apple juice and apple pie spice in a large skillet. Add bananas and cook over medium heat for 2 minutes, basting often.

Combine cornstarch, rum, and flavorings and add to the banana mixture, stirring constantly while cooking for another minute.

Serve immediately over ice cream in individual serving bowls.

Vanilla Beans

With its seductive, honeyed aroma, it shouldn't come as a surprise that vanilla is a potent aphrodisiac. Its tantalizing fragrance excites and arouses the senses. It stirs passion and quickens the blood flow, and stimulates the libido.

It helps to promote inner peace, and some of its other magical properties include love, happiness, and luck.

Cinnamon-Apple Cake

- 1¾ cups sugar, divided
- ½ stick butter, softened
- 1 tsp vanilla extract
- 6 oz fat-free cream cheese, softened (about ¾ cup)
- 2 large eggs
- 1½ cups all-purpose flour
- 1½ tsp baking powder
- 2 tsp ground cinnamon
- 3 cups chopped, peeled Rome apples, or other sweet apples
- Cooking spray

Preheat the oven to 350° F.

Beat 1½ cups sugar, margarine, vanilla, and cream cheese at medium speed until well blended. Add eggs, one at a time, beating well after each addition.

Combine flour, baking powder, and salt. Add to creamed mixture beating at low speed until blended.

Combine ¼ cup sugar and cinnamon. Combine 2 TBSP cinnamon mixture and apples in a bowl and stir the apple mixture into the batter. Pour batter into an 8-inch springform pan coated with cooking spray and sprinkle with remaining cinnamon.

Bake at 350° F for 1 hour and 15 minutes or until the cake pulls away from the sides of the pan. Cool completely on a wire rack and cut using a serrated knife.

You can also make this cake in a 9-inch square cake pan or a 9-inch springform pan; just reduce the cooking time by 5 minutes.

Graham Crackers

Dreaming of crackers may mean you spend too much time looking after other people and neglecting your needs. Do you feel like you are about to crack? Perhaps the pressure is on, and you are struggling to hold it together. What can you do to lighten the load and build up some resistance again?

Another interpretation is that the dream reflects feelings of having to be polite. This could be at work or at home but either way, you feel you have to be welcoming and respectful when you don't necessarily want to be.

Peaches & Cream Pie

- 4 - 5 peaches
- ¼ cup of water
- 1 cup confectioners sugar
- 1 tsp vanilla
- 1 8 oz tub Cool Whip®
- 8 oz cream cheese, softened
- ¼ cup sugar
- 1 graham cracker pie crust

Peel and slice peaches and cook with ¼ cup sugar and ¼ cup water over medium heat for 3 - 4 minutes.

Mix cream cheese, vanilla, and Cool Whip in a medium-size bowl until well blended. Spoon into pie crust, and arrange cooked peaches on top.

Chill in the refrigerator 6 hours before serving.

Vanilla Pudding

Dreaming about eating pudding indicates completion and wholeness. You are ready to share an important part of yourself. Your dream is an omen for spiritual refreshment, tranquility, and renewal. You are getting hooked on something or being hooked in.

Dreaming about eating pudding denotes the aspects of your life that brings about fulfillment and completion. It is time to focus. You are finally Going after what you want in life. The dream represents memories and lessons of the past and the insights that you can still gain. Some protective force is helping you move forward in life.

Southern Style Banana Pudding

- 2 3oz pkgs JELL-O® Vanilla Flavor Cook & Serve Pudding
- 4½ cups milk
- 1 TBSP vanilla extract
- 3 eggs, separated
- Vanilla wafers (about 42)
- 2 large, ripe bananas, sliced
- Dash of cream of tartar
- ¼ cup sugar

Preheat oven to 350° F.

Beat pudding mixes and milk in a medium saucepan with a whisk until blended. Beat egg yolks in a small bowl until blended and gradually stir into the milk mixture. Bring to a full rolling boil over medium heat, stirring constantly. Remove from heat.

Arrange a layer of vanilla wafers on the bottom and up the sides of a 2-quart baking dish. Top with layers of ⅓ pudding and half the banana slices. Repeat layers, keeping the pudding as the final layer.

Beat egg whites and cream of tartar in a medium bowl with a mixer on high speed until foamy. Be patient; it takes a little while. Gradually beat in sugar until peaks form. Spread over pudding, sealing to the edge of the dish.

Bake for 15 minutes or until the meringue is browned. Refrigerate until pudding is set, approximately 4 hours.

Mangos

Associations:

Fire, Air, Mars, Venus, Aries, Sagittarius

Attributes:

Fertility, friendship, happiness, creativity

Drink the juice to enhance fertility. Plant the seed to draw long-term friends back to your side. Wear the blossoms for creativity. Wear mango-scented oil to inspire romance.

Sticky Thai Mango Rice

Yield: 2 Servings

- 1 cup Mahatma® Extra Long Enriched Rice
- 1 cup unsweetened coconut milk
- ¼ cup sugar
- ½ tsp salt
- 2 mangoes, sliced

Cook rice according to package directions.

When rice is almost finished, begin making the coconut milk mixture: combine coconut milk, salt, and sugar in a saucepan and stir until sugar has dissolved. Remove from heat but keep this mixture warm.

Transfer the rice to a large bowl and stir in the coconut milk mixture. Cover and set aside for 30 minutes or until the coconut milk mixture is fully absorbed.

To serve, mold ¼ cup servings of sticky rice onto dessert plates and add freshly sliced mangoes. Top the rice with extra coconut milk.

Witches House Rule #4

Our House is One of Harmony.
No Raised Voices, Except in
Laughter and Song.

Peach Cobbler

Yield: 6 Servings

- 2 cups fresh peaches, sliced, approximately 3 peaches
- ¼ cup butter
- ½ cup flour
- ⅔ cup sugar
- ⅓ cup sugar
- 1 tsp baking powder
- ¼ tsp salt
- ⅓ cup milk
- 1 egg
- ¼ tsp vanilla
- ½ tsp cinnamon
- ¼ cup brown sugar
- Vanilla ice cream for serving (optional)

Preheat the oven to 350°F. While the oven preheats, put the butter in a 9 x 9 glass baking dish and melt in the microwave.

Mix flour, ⅔ cup of sugar, baking powder, and salt in a large bowl. Add milk and egg to the flour mixture and stir to combine. Pour batter over melted butter into the baking dish. Do Not Stir.

Put the peaches in a bowl, and add ⅓ cup sugar along with vanilla and cinnamon. Stir to combine. Spoon peaches gently over the batter, leaving a little space between them. Do Not Stir.

Sprinkle brown sugar over the top of the peaches and batter.

Bake cobbler for 40 - 45 minutes or until the batter is golden brown. Finish with a few minutes on broil to give it a little extra crispness on top (watch closely, so it doesn't burn). Serve warm with vanilla ice cream.

Coconuts

Coconut signals a time of transition and inner reflection, especially if we are feeling restless or unfulfilled. Coconut inspires us to embark on a more profound, meaningful journey within our souls.

The coconut indicates a restless spirit that embarks on epic journeys that inspire the mind, body, and soul to dream big. Coconut challenges us to move beyond our comfort zone to experience something new. They also indicate that a sense of security will follow us on this journey into the unknown.

Coconut Custard Pie

Yield: 6 - 8 Servings

- ½ cup Bisquick®
- ¾ cup sugar
- 4 eggs
- 2 cups milk
- 1 cup flaked coconut
- 1 tsp vanilla
- 1 TBSP butter, softened

Preheat the oven to 400° F.

Combine all ingredients in a large mixing bowl and pour into a 9-inch buttered pie plate. Bake for 25 - 30 minutes or until custard sets. Like magic, it layers into crust, custard, and coconut topping.

Tarot Cards

Swords

Cups

ASSOCIATED WITH THINKING, MATTERS OF THE MIND, INTELLECTUAL / RATIONAL DECISION MAKING (AIR ENERGY)

ASSOCIATED WITH EMOTIONS, MATTERS OF THE HEART (WATER ENERGY)

Pentacles

Wands

ASSOCIATED WITH MATERIAL/FINANCIAL AND PHYSICAL MATTERS: PROSPERITY, ABUNDANCE (EARTH ENERGY)

ASSOCIATED WITH INSPIRATION, CREATIVITY, TRANSFORMATIVE ENDEAVORS (FIRE ENERGY)

Lemon Ricotta Pound Cake

Yield: 8 Servings

- 1½ cups cake flour
- 2½ tsp baking powder
- 1 tsp Kosher salt
- ¾ cups unsalted butter, room temperature, plus more for baking pan
- 1½ cups part-skim Ricotta cheese
- 1½ cups sugar, plus 1 TBSP
- 3 large eggs
- 1 tsp vanilla
- Zest from one lemon
- 2 TBSP fresh lemon juice

Preheat oven to 350° F.

Grease a 9 x 5-inch loaf pan with butter.

In a small bowl, whisk together the flour, baking powder, salt, and lemon zest.

In the bowl of an electric mixer fitted with the paddle attachment, cream the butter, ricotta cheese, and sugar until light and fluffy (approximately 3 minutes). Add each of the eggs, one at a time, while the mixer is running, and blend until incorporated. Mix in the vanilla and lemon juice.

Gradually add the flour mixture and beat until just blended.

Pour batter into prepared pan and bake for 45 - 50 minutes or until the sides begin to pull away from the pan and a toothpick or knife inserted into the middle comes out clean.

Allow to cool in the pan on a wire rack for 10 minutes before turning out of the pan to cool on the wire rack completely.

If desired, dust top with confectioners' sugar.

For a fancier dessert, top with sugared strawberries and whipped cream.

Pumpkin

Samhain is a time to honor those who came before you. Once you're finished with your pumpkin, take it to the woods and leave it as an offering to your ancestors. It also makes excellent deer food!

Make a bird feeder to connect with the spirit of fire and air. Invite winter-friendly birds by making a bird feeder out of your pumpkin. When you notice a bird near it, say a blessing and send him off to carry a wish skyward!

Pumpkin Crisp

Yield: 8 Servings

Filling

- 1 15-oz can of pumpkin puree
- ⅔ cup sugar
- 1 5-oz can evaporated milk
- 3 eggs
- 1 tsp vanilla extract
- 2 tsp pumpkin pie spice
- ¼ teaspoon salt

Topping

- 1 cup crushed gingersnap cookies
- 1 cup quick oats
- ⅓ cup brown sugar
- ¼ teaspoon baking soda
- ¼ teaspoon baking powder
- ½ cup butter, softened

Preheat oven to 350°F.

Grease a deep square 2-3 quart baking dish.

In a large bowl, whisk together all of the filling ingredients; pour them into the prepared dish.

In a medium bowl, combine the crushed gingersnap cookies, oats, brown sugar, baking soda, and baking powder. Then, use a fork to incorporate the butter into the dry mixture.

Evenly sprinkle the topping over the pumpkin filling.

Bake for 35 - 45 minutes, or until the center of the pumpkin pie filling reaches 175°F. The center will still have a little wiggle, but it won't be super runny.

Top with vanilla ice cream or whipped cream, if desired.

Chocolate

Use chocolate in love spells to help with self-love, finding love, feeling in love, feeling happy, and feeling content.

Hot chocolate was shared by couples in marriage ceremonies and used as an aphrodisiac. It was a spell inducer, especially for sex and romance. Chocolate was thought to be the blood, essence, and vitality of life. Men drank chocolate "for success with the women," and women drank it for rejuvenation during childbirth and menopause.

Chocolate Crinkle Cookies

- 1 cup unsweetened cocoa powder (sift if it's lumpy)
- 2 cups all-purpose flour
- 1½ tsp baking powder
- ¼ tsp salt
- ⅓ cup butter, softened
- 1½ cups sugar
- 1 tsp vanilla
- 4 large eggs
- ½ cup powdered sugar

Combine dry ingredients: Cocoa powder, flour, baking powder, and salt in a medium bowl. Set aside.

Cream wet ingredients: Place butter, sugar, and vanilla in a large mixing bowl and beat with an electric mixer until combined. Add the eggs, one at a time, and mix on medium-low speed just until combined – about 10 seconds each.

Make the cookie dough: Add the dry ingredients to the egg mixture and mix on low speed until incorporated.

Chill cookie dough: Cover the bowl and chill the dough for at least 1 hour or up to overnight (the longer you chill, the thicker the cookies will be).

Roll cookies: When ready to bake, preheat the oven to 350°F. Place the powdered sugar in a medium bowl. Roll the dough into tablespoon-sized balls and cover them well with the sugar.

Bake cookies: Place on a lined baking sheet with enough space between them (bake in batches) and bake for 10 - 15 minutes, or until balls of dough spread and crackle. Cookies will still be soft, so let them cool on the baking sheet for 5 minutes before removing them to a cooling rack to cool completely.

Strawberries

Associations:

Feminine,
Venus, Water,
Aphrodite

Attributes:

Love and
luck

Birthmarks in the shape of strawberries were thought to be signs that the person bearing the mark was a witch.

Carry strawberry leaves in a pouch to bring luck and love.
Use in sachets or incense to enhance love in your life.

Strawberry Vanilla Poke Cake

Yield: 6 Servings

- 1 box white cake mix
- 2 cups fresh strawberries chopped
- 1 11-oz jar of strawberry syrup (ice cream topping)
- 2 cups heavy cream
- ½ cup sour cream
- ½ cup confectioner's sugar
- 1 tsp vanilla extract
- ½ cup pretzels crushed

Cake:

Prepare cake mix and bake according to package directions.

Poke holes in prepared cake with the handle of a wooden spoon. Pour strawberry syrup over cake and spread; making sure you fill the holes with syrup. Chill in the refrigerator for an hour.

Topping:

In a medium mixing bowl combine heavy cream, sour cream, vanilla extract and powdered sugar. Blend with a hand mixer until stiff peaks form. Spread the topping over the chilled cake.

Top with chopped fresh strawberries and crushed pretzels.

Always throw spilled *Salt* over your left shoulder;

Keep *Rosemary* growing by your garden gate;

Plant *Lavender* for Luck; and

Fall in *Love* whenever you can.

So mote it be,
Eilish and *Anya*

CREDITS and RESOURCES

Illustrations by Dawné Dominque (DusktilDawnDesigns.com) created with:
Vectorstock.com
Depositphoto.com
iStock.com
Canstock.com
Pond5.com
Bigstock.com
FreeVintageIllustrations.com
PublicDomainPics.com
Clip Art From Bloomella.com
PNGTree.com
Etsy.com:
- bloomella.com
- Tasyl Studio
- kennasatodesigns.etsy.com

Recipe Credits by Amy Smith:
The recipes contained in the book are a combination of my creations, as well as recipes that have been passed down through the family over generations with the original origins unknown. Recipes from the sources below were collected through the years and were adapted to suit my taste or remain as originally written.

Southern Living/Oxmoor House
Home Chef
The Enchanted Broccoli Forest by Mollie Katzen
Giada De Laurentiis
Cooking Light
The Vegetarian Epicure
The Joy of Cooking
Mrs. Rowe's Restaurant Cookbook
Pinterest & Cooking blogs

Research Sources for Grimoire Information by Emily Bex
Internet:
Dreamsopedia.com
Pinterest.com
Wikipedia.com
Witchapedia.com
The Magick Kitchen Blog
Numerous Witchcraft Blogs

Books:
Susan Greenwood. *The Illustrated Encyclopedia of Witchcraft & Practical Magic*
Anness Publishing Ltd. ©2015
Arin Murphy-Hiscock. *Spellcrafting*, Adams Media ©2020
Susan Greenwood. *The Encyclopedia of Magic* Hermes House

Publishing ©2001
Ann Moura. *Grimoire for the Green Witch: A Complete Book of Shadows*,
Llewellyn Publications ©2003